# Good Housekeeping
## Consumer Guide

# You and Your Rights

# Good Housekeeping
## Consumer Guide

# You and Your Rights

Suzanne Wilkinson &

Patricia Schofield

EBURY PRESS · LONDON

First published in 1995

1 3 5 7 9 10 8 6 4 2

Copyright 1995 © Random House UK Limited or the National Magazine Company Limited

Suzanne Wilkinson and Patricia Schofield have asserted
their right to be identified as the authors of this work.

All rights reserved. No part of this publication may be reproduced, stored in a retrieval system,
or transmitted in any form or by any means, electronic, mechanical, photocopying, recording
or otherwise, without the prior permission of the copyright owner.

The expression GOOD HOUSEKEEPING as used in the title of this book is the trade mark
of the National Magazine Company Limited and the Hearst Corporation, registered in the
United Kingdom and USA, and other principal countries of the world, and is the absolute
property of the National Magazine Company Limited and the Hearst Corporation. The use
of this trade mark other than with the express permission of the National Magazine Company
Limited or the Hearst Corporation is strictly prohibited.

First published in the United Kingdom in 1995 by
Ebury Press · Random House · 20 Vauxhall Bridge Road · London SW1V 2SA

Random House Australia (Pty) Limited
20 Alfred Street · Milsons Point · Sydney · New South Wales 2061 · Australia

Random House New Zealand Limited
18 Poland Road · Glenfield
Auckland 10 · New Zealand

Random House South Africa (Pty) Limited
PO Box 337 · Bergvlei · South Africa

Random House UK Limited Reg. No. 954009

A CIP catalogue record for this book is available from the British Library.

Editor: Alison Wormleighton
Design: Martin Lovelock

ISBN: 0 09 180703 4

Printed and bound in Great Britain by Mackays of Chatham, plc.

Note: All prices quoted are approximate
and correct at the time of going to press

# Contents

# Chapter 1

# The Law

Most of this book deals with the law, its practical applications and what you can do to ensure your rights. This chapter covers the mechanics of the system – where and how you can achieve your rights. In other words, it explains the framework within which you will have to work, answering questions like: Do I need expert advice? Where will my case be heard? Will I be able to afford it? Other areas dealt with in this chapter include:

- alternatives to traditional courts
- paying for legal action
- what you can expect from your solicitor and what to do if you don't get it

Even though the book begins with the court structure, going to court should in fact be a last resort in a dispute. It is extremely costly and time-consuming.

## THE COUNTY COURTS

The county courts' primary function is to recover money. It could be because of a breach of contract between you and the debtor (such as a

---

### The court structure

The courts of England and Wales are divided into civil and criminal. Civil courts include the county courts and the High Court. Ninety per cent of all civil proceedings take place in the county courts, which are local courts. Criminal trials take place in magistrates' courts and Crown Courts. This means that cases of different degrees of seriousness are heard in different courts and if you want to appeal you can have your appeal heard in the next court up the scale.

company which took your money but failed to do the agreed work, or a dishonoured cheque you received for goods or services). Claims for damages (for example, the dry-cleaning company that ruined your suit), trespass or negligence also fall into this category. County courts will hear cases up to £50,000 and you can start proceedings in any county court.

All money-only claims are started by **default summons**, which can be for either a fixed or an unfixed amount. Actions which are not money-only claims are started by **fixed date summons**. These usually involve matters like disputes between neighbours, or landlord-and-tenant cases.

## Small claims

Within the county courts there is a distinct procedure called small claims, which is for smaller debt recovery and breach of contract. There is no small claims court as such, although we frequently refer to it. The concept behind small claims is that it is a simple system, not as formal as the mainstream county courts, and therefore individuals can take their own action to court. By working within the county court system, should a case become more complex than originally envisaged it can be directed back into the main civil system. This is an unlikely event in most small claims. Generally cases are heard in the district where the incidents happened or where the defendant carries on business or resides.

Use the small claims procedure for disputes of £1,000 or less. You can include actual loss and consequential loss such as the cost of hiring a car whilst yours was out of action, or using the launderette whilst you were waiting for your washing machine to be repaired.

The procedure is kept as simple as possible:
- District judges do not wear wigs or gowns. They like to be addressed as 'Sir' or 'Madam'.
- A lay person should be able to manage his or her own case.
- Hearings are heard in private.
- Forms are written in straightforward English.
- Most of the procedure can be dealt with by post, apart from the hearing itself.

- It is unusual for a judge to award any sort of costs order at the end of the proceedings.

## How to obtain judgement for a debt

1  Before you prepare your summons, send a 'final letter before action', stating that you intend to start court proceedings. This may be necessary at a later date to ensure you can claim court fees and interest. Many debtors do pay up when they receive a final letter before action.

2  Be clear in your own mind as to who the defendant is – in other words, exactly whom you are suing. You can sue more than one person with regard to the same matter if there is a case against each one. This should be stated when you prepare your summons. As well as suing individuals you can also sue businesses, organisations and authorities. Service of a summons need no longer be at the registered office of a limited company. It can be where the company trades, for example, a high street branch.

3  Pick up the relevant forms from any county court. These forms are free and are prefixed with the letter N. You will find county courts listed under Courts in phone books. Prescribed forms are compulsory; practice forms are not. If you are filling in any forms you need three copies – one for yourself, one for the court and one for the court to send to the person you are suing. Photocopies will do.

4  When you issue a summons you have to pay a fee on a sliding scale, depending on the amount of your claim. This fee is recoverable from the defendant if you win. The forms can be sent by ordinary post to the court

---

### The virtue of patience

To most people the law is ridiculously slow. There are consistent delays and set procedures to go through within the court system so that you can never get things resolved as quickly as you would like. To this end a Courts Citizen's Charter was launched in July 1991 by John Major covering all county courts. You can't, however, claim financial compensation if you feel that the experience you've encountered fails to achieve the standards set, so its usefulness is questionable.

---

**Tip**

You can commence court proceedings in any county court, but bear in mind where the defendant's home court is. If he defends the summons then the case will automatically be transferred to his home court. The file will be sent by post to that court, which can lead to delay and/or loss of the file. It is easier to file the summons in your own court if you think the defendant will not file a defence; but if you think you are in for a fight, it will avoid an extra stage if you start proceedings in his court.

---

or delivered in person. If you take them yourself you can get them checked and corrected immediately if needs be. You will have to fill in the names and addresses of those involved, particulars of the claim and any interest (in the case of debt).

**5** Serve the summons on the defendant. This is normally done by post by the court. Service is deemed to have been effective seven days after posting in the case of an individual or partnership and two days after posting in the case of a company. If the defendant proves elusive or the letter is returned undelivered, you can use bailiffs (around £10) or a process server or private detective, or 'serve' it yourself personally.

**6** The debtor has a choice. Within 14 days he must decide on either:
- to pay in full
- to admit the whole claim or part of it, giving details of his financial situation and making an offer of payment
- to deny the claim, with or without bringing his own counter claim.

If the summons is defended and your claim is for £1,000 or less, then on receipt of a defence the claim will automatically be referred to

---

**County court fees**

To issue a summons for the recovery of money

| | |
|---|---|
| Not more than £600 | £10 (minimum fee) |
| Exceeding £600 but not exceeding £1,000 | £65 |
| Exceeding £1,000 but not exceeding £5,000 | £70 |
| Exceeding £5,000 | £80 |

**Remember**

If you receive a summons, do not ignore it. Unpaid judgement debts can affect your future credit rating.

arbitration. This is known as the small claims procedure. If it is for more than £1,000 it can still go to arbitration if you both agree or the court orders it. If a counter claim is filed, it is advisable to file a defence to the counter claim.

If it is not defended then you can apply to the court to have judgement automatically given in your favour. This is called **judgement in default** and enables you to request payment straight away. Unfortunately, this involves you in more form-filling. However, getting money out of debtors is never as easy as it sounds. (*See* How to enforce judgement for a debt, page 12)

The case will automatically go to trial if it is a more complex issue or where fraud is alleged against a party. Circuit judges hear larger cases in the county court and in the Crown Court.

7  Nearly all small claims hearings are automatically transferred to the defendant's court, which involves you in more time and expense if it is a distance away. You can ask the court to have the case heard in your local court but you will need to give the district judge reasons to support your application. You will usually be given a 14-day time limit before the hearing, when each side should send to the other copies of documents to support their case and details of witnesses' reports.

8  Your preparation is the most important part. It will pay dividends to take time to get your evidence together to support your claim or defence. Recollections differ so arm yourself with witnesses, expert witnesses, faulty goods or documents or photos if appropriate. Many people attend court convinced that they are in the right. If the case has gone as far as a hearing, the other side think they are right too. There is bound to be a conflicting version of events. The law operates on the basis that it is up to the plaintiff to prove his or her case on the balance of probabilities. This contrasts with criminal law where it must be proved without reasonable doubt who is the guilty party. Here the decision can be made even though the situation is not so clear-cut.

**9** Hearings take place between 10 am and 4 pm weekdays. Most hearings take one or two hours and you'll have a decision by the end which is confirmed in writing later. The judgement is called the award. If the plaintiff wins he will get costs and expenses (such as loss of earnings and the cost of travel and experts' reports) but at fairly modest rates. In the case of debt, interest will be added at the appropriate rate. The amount of the award must be based on recommendations in law.

**10** You can appeal but only if you can prove that the judge or arbitrator was wrong on a point of law or that there was prejudice or misconduct.

**Northern Ireland and Scotland** have equivalents to the small claims court, but there are some differences.

In Northern Ireland a small claim is made by obtaining an Application for Arbitration from your local county court. No costs or other expenses are awarded but you will get back your court fee if you win.

In Scotland the claim limit is £750 and the case is heard by a sheriff in the sheriff court. There is a preliminary hearing too to make the actual hearing more streamlined. Expenses of up to £75 are awarded to the winner only in defended cases involving claims of more than £200.

**How to enforce judgement for a debt**

Do make sure that it is worth pursuing this further. If the debtor has no means and assets then there is nothing to be had and you are simply left to cover the debt yourself, unsatisfactory as this outcome is. Check to see whether a company is in liquidation. Check to see how many other judgements there are against the defendant, by contacting Registry Trust Ltd. There is a small charge (£4 in person and £4.50 by post) for the search. If you think the defendant may dispose of his assets you may have to consider what is known as a Mareva injunction and for this you will need to employ a solicitor.

If it is worth pursuing, consider what method of enforcement you will use:

- **A warrant of execution** is the most common. The debtor's goods can be seized and sold, usually at public auction, to cover the amount of the judgement plus costs of execution. This is executed by a county court bailiff, after you have completed another form called Request for Warrant of Execution and would relate to movable property and leases. It does not apply to goods on HP or real property. Often the arrival of the bailiff produces the money. If the judgement is for £5,000 or more, then it will be handled by the High Court and is carried out by the sheriff's officers. It is called a Writ of FiFa, but be warned: High Court costs go up substantially.

- **A charging order** relates to land or, occasionally, stocks. This will involve you in more hearings in the High Court (for sums over £5,000) or in a county court (for amounts under £5,000). This is referred to as a county court judgement.

- **A garnishee order** attaches a debt owed by a third party (the garnishee) to the judgement debtor which is to be paid directly to the creditor.

- **An attachment of earnings order** is available only in a county court. The order is directed to the employer of the debtor to deduct a specific amount from the employee's wages which is paid to the court for the judgement creditor. It obviously cannot be applied to earnings from self- employment or when the debtor is unemployed. It is only effective if the debtor is in stable long-term employment.

- **Appointment of receiver by way of equitable execution** is used when other methods fail. The court may appoint a receiver, who will

| Examples of county court fees to enforce judgement for a debt | |
|---|---|
| Warrant of execution 15p in the £ | minimum £10 |
| | maximum £50 |
| Charging order | |
| (diverting money held by the debtor) | £25 |
| Garnishee order | |
| (securing the debt against the debtor's home) | £25 |
| Attachment of earnings fee | |
| (the court equivalent of PAYE) 10p in the £ | minimum £10 |
| | maximum £80 |

be able to get payment from the assets specified in the order. The assets may include money in joint accounts and life assurance policies.

## CRIMINAL LAW

You may inadvertently get involved in the criminal law through a minor traffic offence, a parking offence or as the victim of rape.

For the offence to be classed as criminal, there has to be a crime committed against an identifiable person for an identifiable crime. Any investigation is begun by the police. When they feel they have gathered sufficient evidence and are ready to charge, or if they want advice, it is referred to the Crown Prosecution Service (CPS). Once someone has appeared in court for the first time then the case is taken over by the CPS. The role of the investigation team – the police – is very different from that of the prosecution team. The CPS makes the ultimate decision and can overrule the police. Many people become confused about this distinction, and there is a Public Enquiry Point on 0171-334 8505.

Over 95 per cent of criminal cases are completed in the magistrates' court. The remaining trials take place in the Crown Court.

- If it is a **summary offence** – such as drunk and disorderly and common assault – it is heard in a magistrates' court.
- When a case – for example, an actual bodily harm assault (ABH) or theft – is **triable either way** the defendant can opt for trial in either the magistrates' court or the Crown Court.
- An **indictable offence** such as grievous bodily harm, murder, rape will be committed or transferred to the Crown Court.

Sometimes cases are discontinued. Possible reasons for this include the defendant dying, anticipated forensic or other evidence failing to materialise, witnesses deciding not to give evidence after all or the defendant being imprisoned for a more serious offence.

### Magistrates' courts

At a first appearance, for example for a road traffic offence, if the defendant pleads guilty and any necessary documents, e.g. a driving licence, are shown in court, the case can usually be dealt with straight away. If the plea is 'not guilty', a trial date is set so that the prosecution and defence can organise the calling of witnesses.

The length of time allocated for a trial depends upon how many witnesses will be called and whether an interpreter will be needed, which would slow down proceedings. There is no pre-set limit for the number of witnesses. For a traffic accident, for example, six or seven witnesses might be called and the hearing might be allocated one or two days. If a trial takes longer than anticipated and is only part-heard then it can be reconvened another day, but courts try to avoid this.

In the majority of cases the prosecuting side is the Crown Prosecution Service because the police have been involved. However, for an issue concerning, say, noise the environmental health department of the local authority may be the prosecutor, or in a private dispute it might be a neighbour. If a victim decides to take out a private prosecution, they need to get a court to issue a summons. They can either represent themselves or instruct a solicitor or barrister. The CPS has the opportunity, if contacted, of deciding to take the case over or letting it proceed.

Lay magistrates are unpaid volunteers. There are 30,000 lay justices compared with about 90 stipendiary magistrates who are paid, and who are qualified members of the legal profession.

Magistrates have a range of sentencing powers. They can fine up to £5,000 or impose a custodial sentence of up to 6 months. They can make a conditional or absolute discharge, or a community or probation order. The maximum sentence available for specific offences is set down in law.

In all judgements, mitigating and aggravating circumstances will be considered. Mitigating circumstances may include whether it was a first offence, whether an early guilty plea has been made and the offender's circumstances. Examples of aggravating circumstances are a string of previous similar convictions or the seriousness of the offence.

Appeals are rare: less than 2 per cent of cases heard in the magistrates' court appeal. Appeals go forward to the Crown Court, where a judge sits with two magistrates who have not been involved in the first trial.

## FAMILY COURTS

The Children Act 1989, which came into force in 1991, is unique in setting up, for the first time, a concurrent jurisdiction between the three levels of court (magistrates', county and High Court).

### Magistrates' court:

• Many private law cases (excluding divorce) can commence in magistrates' courts, although more complex private law cases can commence in the county courts or even in the High Court.

Magistrates, sitting in magistrates' courts (also known as family proceedings courts), hear cases in both private and public law. They are selected from special family proceedings panels. There are 358 of these panels in England and Wales but the number of magistrates on each panel varies. *See* Assistance by way of representation (ABWOR), page 25.

### County court:

• There are now four distinct forms of county court, with varying jurisdictions in family cases. Non-divorce county courts have no jurisdiction apart from making domestic violence injunctions. Divorce county courts can issue all private law proceedings under the Children Act, but contested matters have to be transferred to family hearing centres. These are able to hear all private law matters, but have no public law jurisdiction. Care centres have full jurisdiction in both types of law.

### High Court:

• The High Court has jurisdiction to hear all cases relating to children, and it exercises an exclusive jurisdiction in wardship. Under the Act the local authority has a right to apply to the High Court for the exercise of this jurisdiction, having obtained leave from the court.

All the judiciary involved in Children Act proceedings, from magistrates through district and circuit judges to High Court judges, have been chosen for their special interest in family proceedings. They must have received special training before undertaking any of the work.

### Appearing as a witness

- A leaflet explaining the procedures involved will be sent to you before you have to go to court.
- Take all papers you have about the case with you.
- Be prepared to wait. Take a book or magazine.
- If you are a victim of crime, someone from the Victim Support scheme may go with you. Victim Support also runs the Witness Service which offers support and information to victims and witnesses in the Crown Court. Contact the National Office for details.
- If you are concerned about meeting 'the other side' tell the usher when you arrive. Ask the receptionist if there is a separate room to wait in.
- If you are nervous you might find it useful to look at the courtroom before your case starts. Visit in the early morning or at lunchtime or sit in the public gallery and listen to other cases.
- If you have made a statement, you will want to refresh your memory so make sure you have a copy before going to court.
- You may be familiar with the case, but others won't, so don't leave out any evidence.
- You can claim for travel expenses, meal allowances and lost earnings. Ask for a claim form from the caseworker at Crown Courts. For magistrates' courts, the forms are sent out prior to court attendance via the CPS or Crime Support Group.
- Be sure you answer the questions as fully and as accurately as possible.

# ALTERNATIVES TO TRADITIONAL COURTS

As costs rise exorbitantly, the law is becoming increasingly unavailable to ordinary people. If they are in employment, they are unlikely to get help with Legal Aid (*see* Meeting the cost of legal action, page 23) and so other alternatives such as arbitration, ombudsmen and tribunals are increasingly being encouraged. The only other alternative is DIY litigation.

### Arbitration

Both sides will want to resolve a dispute quickly with minimum expense and this is what arbitration aims to do. It is the process by which two parties in dispute agree to appoint a third, independent person to resolve their differences. It is the only alternative if the parties want a final and legally binding decision without all the formalities of going to court. Arbitration has several advantages over a court hearing. It is private, the rules of evidence are not strictly applied and the procedure is informal.

You might try arbitration with a trade association to resolve a dispute on, say, a sofa that has not worn as well as you would have expected. Arbitration is unsuited to establishing rights or making an order which needs to be enforced (for example, a dispute over possession of land) or to children's cases. To find out whether arbitration is possible, first find out whether the company is part of an association which has an arbitration scheme in place.

In the mid 70s the Office of Fair Trading set up these Consumer Dispute Resolution schemes. For details of the procedure to follow and of various schemes, contact the Chartered Institute of Arbitrators.

The main advantage of arbitration is speed in getting the proceedings underway, and in the proceedings themselves. In most cases arbitration should be complete within 14 weeks (though it has recently been accused of having lost its informality and speed and becoming too much like the litigation it was set up to replace).

---

### Conciliation

Sometimes referred to as mediation, conciliation is still in its infancy, but the principle is sound. The aim is to bring the warring parties together with a conciliator, in the hope that by talking things through, in the presence of a third party, the parties can resolve their point(s) of difference. It is often used in divorce proceedings (with regard to dividing up the matrimonial home) and in cross-border, local authority disputes and commercial disputes. A lot less expensive and quicker than going to court, conciliation should take no longer than a few weeks to arrange a day to conduct. If this conciliation does not result in settlement arbitration can follow as a matter of course.

Arbitration will usually involve only one arbitrator although there can be more. (In a tribunal there is always more than one arbitrator; often there are up to three.) It costs £117.50 to appoint an arbitrator and then a further fee for the hearing itself which can be from £40 to over £100 per hour depending on the arbitrator. Arbitrators are appointed by the Institute of Arbitrators and are totally independent. They will usually be experts in the field of the dispute, with knowledge of the law, unlike a judge who is an expert only in matters of law.

If a small claim is involved, then arbitration will be quick and documentation only will be required.

An ABTA case can typically take five to six hours, a FIMBRA case may take days, while something involving the NHBC might only consist of a site inspection, just as it would in court. The Institute of Arbitrators will ensure that there is a timetable and it gives you some means of enforcement.

The aim has been to give the arbitrator powers which ensure maximum flexibility of procedure and hence economic resolution of the dispute. In nine out of ten cases legal representation is not necessary so costs are kept to a minimum. The winner usually gets their registration fee (around £25) refunded by the loser and sometimes a discretionary award.

Because they know the limits of what they will have to pay if they lose, many trade associations have codes of conduct for their members which offer arbitration to the public if they are dissatisfied with the outcome of a complaint and want to take matters further. Each trade association which operates such a scheme has its own agreement with the Institute and in many cases the trade association will bear a lot of the costs.

## Ombudsmen

These were established to investigate complaints about service, bad administration and abuses of powers by government departments and public sector bodies. There are now a wide range of ombudsman schemes in both the public and private sector and more are constantly being added.

Before approaching an ombudsman you must complain to the organisation directly in writing first so that they are given a reasonable opportunity to deal with it. Using an ombudsman scheme to sort out a complaint or dispute may be an alternative to going to court as the schemes are free and aim to be less time-consuming.

Ombudsmen have nevertheless been criticised for not going far enough in helping to resolve disputes. For example, not all ombudsmen can make decisions which are binding on organisations, and yet there is such a tremendous imbalance of power between an individual and a large organisation. Each scheme varies in the type of complaint it handles, the power it has and the procedures it uses. In some schemes there is the provision for the ombudsman to make a monetary award.

- They operate independently to investigate complaints from individuals against private or public organisations.
- They decide whether there has been maladministration such as unreasonable delay, neglect, inaction, inefficiency, failure to follow policy etc., and what the outcome should be.
- If you are still dissatisfied you may have the right to proceed with a court hearing or arbitration if the other side agrees.
- By being in effect watchdogs, they make recommendations about improved procedures or practices for the future.

Ombudsmen operate in the following areas: banks, building societies, estate agents, government departments, insurance companies, legal services, local authorities, national health service, pensions, investment, funerals. Before you begin putting a complaint in writing, phone them for any information available and any special forms.

**Tribunals**
Tribunals operate extensively. Usually a lawyer is chairman and two lay

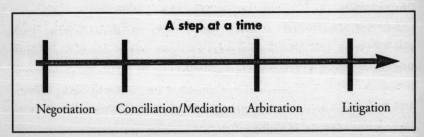

**A step at a time**

Negotiation   Conciliation/Mediation   Arbitration   Litigation

advisers sit with him. Legal Aid is available for only a minority of tribunals. In many cases, therefore, the applicant must either attempt to get advice and representation from free legal sources such as law centres and Citizens' Advice Bureaux or pay for representation or do without.

The matters decided by tribunals often concern rights to welfare benefits; the right to remain in the country; pensions appeals, appeals against DSS decisions relating to war pensions, the disabled, widows and/or children; VAT and duties; detention under mental health legislation; unfair dismissal from work; compensation for compulsory land purchase; and council tax appeals. The case law in these areas is usually highly complex.

The Council on Tribunals is an independent advisory body. Although it cannot deal with individual complaints about a tribunal decision or about the conduct of a tribunal, it will take note of defects in the procedures of tribunals.

### Trade unions

If you have a dispute at work or some other problem involving the workplace, such as redundancy, trade unions will assist if you are a member.

# FREE LEGAL ADVICE

### Law centres

The first was established in the early 1970s and there are now around 55 usually found in inner-city areas. They are normally funded by the local authority. Lawyers and advice workers who have some legal qualifications provide the service for modest remuneration and at no cost to clients.

Law centres specialise in areas that are not well represented in the private sector and for which legal aid is unavailable, such as housing problems, immigration, welfare rights, health and employment. They provide a high level of expertise at tribunals, where they will represent you, and at social security tribunals and are often more specialised and therefore more knowledgeable than private solicitors.

The co-ordinating body for law centres, the Law Centres Federation, will supply a list of your local law centres.

### Citizens' Advice Bureaux (CAB)

These are funded by the relevant local authority. Their areas of speciality lie in social security, such as appeals, pensions, national insurance, child benefit. Debt is also a major issue on which they advise. Employment rights such as unfair dismissal and industrial tribunal procedures represent a large area of their work. Consumer issues such as double glazing, second-hand cars and building work are dealt with mainly by phone. Often this type of inquiry is from a consumer who needs to be pointed in the right direction but can help themselves. Family and personal matters are often further down the list, but CABx are covering wider and wider arenas.

Housing Advice Centres deal with issues like landlord and tenant rights, leasehold rights and mortgage repossessions.

The address of your local CAB can be found in the phone directory. It offers lots of free useful information that you can take away, so is useful as the first port of call. CABx usually operate by giving you some generalised information when you appear and following this up with a more detailed appointment if you need it. All advice is free.

### The Free Representation Unit (FRU)

CABx often have access to FRU to help the individual get free representation. Running since the early 70s, FRU was set up by members of the Bar. It deals only with cases sent to it by other advice agencies such as CABx or law centres. Its representatives are qualified barristers or bar students and pupil barristers. Its effectiveness is limited by the number of bar students willing to volunteer, but it does play a useful part in tribunals where legal aid is not available.

### Charters

Since you cannot vote with your feet and take your business elsewhere when you are dissatisfied with a government organisation, there are published charters concerning levels of service. The Citizen's Charter aims to raise the standard of public services and make them more responsive to the needs and wishes of the people who use them. Charters tell you about the services they cover, what standards you can expect from a particular organisation and what to do if you have a complaint, but they are not the complaints line themselves. For a list of the 40 charters published by individual services, phone the Citizen's Charter Publications line. Charters cover areas such as employment, road users, passengers, parents, patients and The Child Support Agency charter. Since January 1993 when the Courts Charter was introduced, hundreds of thousands of pounds' compensation has been paid to people who suffered financial loss because of errors and delays by staff.

## MEETING THE COST OF LEGAL ACTION

Because legal action is so expensive, and relatively few people are eligible for Legal Aid, many families who take a case to court end up out of pocket even if they win since winners may have to pay some of their own fees. If they lose they may have to pay the other side's costs as well as their own.

In most towns there are solicitors who carry out Legal Aid work. You can get their names from your Citizens' Advice Bureau, a law centre or the phone book, or you can get Legal Aid advice from Legal Aid head office.

When you see your solicitor, he or she will tell you whether you have a case to fight and what sort of help you need. This initial advice comes under the category of the **Green Form Scheme** but to get it you have to qualify on financial grounds. Many cases can be resolved under the Green Form Scheme (so-called because it involves filling in a green form!) as a lot of people just need straightforward advice from a solicitor. But if your case is more complicated, or if it has to go to court, your solicitor may then advise you to take the matter further and apply for Civil Legal Aid or Criminal Legal Aid depending on the type of case. If you are successful and you get money or property with the help of Legal Aid you may be asked to contribute towards your solicitor's bill. This is called the **statutory charge**. In this way Legal Aid acts as a loan.

## The criteria for Legal Aid

Legal Aid was designed to help the less well-off, though fewer and fewer people are eligible, as the Legal Aid bill has rocketed in recent years. Whether you qualify or not depends on your financial position. Your income and savings must be low. If you and a partner live as husband and wife, your partner's income and savings will be counted along with your own (unless the case is a dispute between the two of you).

What you have after paying for expenses such as deductions and dependants is called disposable income. If this is £70 or less a week you will qualify for free help under the Green Form Scheme. For Civil Legal Aid the limits are different and more allowances are made for expenses, such as rent or mortgage. Your disposable income for Civil Legal Aid must be £7,060 a year or less.

Your savings must be below £1,000 for help under the Green Form Scheme and below £6,750 for Civil Legal Aid. (Pensioners applying for Civil Legal Aid are allowed to have more savings than this.)

The only exceptions to these limits are in personal injury cases (such as accidents at work or medical negligence where your health has suffered as a result) where you would be allowed to have £7,780 in disposable income and £8,560 in savings.

The Legal Aid Board administers Legal Aid under the general guidance of the Lord Chancellor. For this purpose, England and Wales are divided into a number of areas. Each area has a Legal Aid office and an area committee made up of practising solicitors and barristers. The area office decides whether your application for Civil Legal Aid satisfies the merits test. The area committee deals with appeals against refusals of Legal Aid.

For information on similar schemes in Scotland and Northern Ireland. write to the Scottish Legal Aid Board or the  Law Society of Northern Ireland.

## Service provided by Legal Aid

There are three elements to the Legal Aid scheme:

**1** Legal Advice and Assistance – often referred to as the Green Form Scheme. As its name implies, only assistance and no representation is provided (*see* page 23).

**2** ABWOR – this covers the cost of a solicitor preparing your case and representing you in most civil cases in Family Proceedings Courts. These cases include separation, maintenance (except child maintenance, where the Child Support Agency has jurisdiction), residence/contact, paternity and defended adoption proceedings. It is also available to review-patients before Mental Health Review Tribunals, to prisoners facing disciplinary charges before the prison governor and to discretionary lifers whose cases are referred to the parole board. ABWOR is available through your solicitor, who will fill in the appropriate form which will be submitted to the relevant Legal Aid office.

The income and capital conditions for ABWOR are different to Legal Advice and Assistance. You will qualify for ABWOR if your weekly disposable income is £153 or less and you have savings under £3,000. There is no means test for Mental Health Review Tribunal cases. You may have to pay a contribution for ABWOR.

3 Civil Legal Aid – this covers all the work leading up to and including the court proceedings, as well as representation by a solicitor and, if necessary, a barrister. For some proceedings involving children, Legal Aid is granted without a means test. It is available for cases in:

- the House of Lords, High Court and Court of Appeal
- county courts where you intend to sue a retailer for faulty goods, a doctor for negligence or an employer for an accident at work (but not judgement summonses nor, usually, the decree proceedings for undefended divorce and judicial separation)
- Family proceedings courts about marriage and the family, including

---

### Help in an emergency

Everyone is entitled to free legal advice if they are questioned by the police whether they have been arrested or not. This legal help is available whatever your income. Ask to see your solicitor or the duty solicitor.

You are also entitled to free legal advice on your first appearance at a magistrates' court, whatever your income. Ask to see the duty solicitor. But if you have time it is much better to apply for Legal Aid before you go to the magistrates' court so that your solicitor is prepared.

separation, maintenance (except child maintenance, where the Child Support Agency has jurisdiction), residence/contact and defended adoption proceedings – although these are also covered by ABWOR
- the Employment Appeal Tribunal
- the Lands Tribunal
- the Commons Commissioners
- the Restrictive Practices Court (for some cases)
  Civil Legal Aid is *not* available for proceedings before a coroner's court and most tribunals (except those listed above), nor for proceedings involving libel and slander.

## Criminal Legal Aid

If you have been charged with a criminal offence in some cases you can apply for Criminal Legal Aid. This will pay some or all of the cost of a solicitor to prepare your case before you go to court and a barrister to represent you in court.

Criminal Legal Aid is not available to bring a private prosecution – that is, bringing a criminal case against another person – although this is unlikely to happen because usually the case against you is brought by the Crown Prosecution Service. However, you are entitled to free legal advice on first appearance at a magistrates' court.

## Choosing a solicitor

There are so many areas of law that it is wise to find a solicitor who specialises in the appropriate area, be it personal injury, family, property disputes, environmental, health service, local authority issues, you can ring The Law Society or visit the reference section of your local library – *Chambers & Partners Law Directory*, the Legal 500 or the Law Society's regional directories will give you lists of firms and their specialist areas. A useful booklet, *Getting the Best from your Solicitor*, is available from the National Consumer Council.

## Legal expenses insurance

You can get insurance which will help cover you for certain legal expenses.

It may be included in your car or home insurance policy, or for an extra premium you may be able to add it on. Separate policies are also available.

- As with other insurance policies you have to disclose in writing all relevant facts when taking out or renewing a policy.
- There are usually strict time limits for reporting claims.
- Often the companies offer telephone legal advice.
- You need at least £10,000 in legal fees cover.
- The insurance company will only support you if they think you have a good chance of winning.

## COMPLAINTS AGAINST SOLICITORS

It is exceedingly difficult to get any retribution against a solicitor for overcharging or negligence. You need persistence and determination.

The Solicitors' Complaints Bureau (SCB) was created in 1986 to separate the investigation of complaints about solicitors from the Law

---

### Paying your own way

Even if you are eligible for Legal Aid, you must ask your solicitor about costs. He is professionally obliged to give you the best information about likely costs. Be sure to cover the following questions/points:

- How much do you charge?
  (Privately £60–£75 per hour and for Legal Aid work they get £45–£100) Costs will vary depending on the work. For example, attendance at court can be one rate, letter-writing another, but you should try to get some idea.
- How many hours are likely to be involved?
- Will there be additional costs like a barrister or expert witnesses which will significantly affect the cost?
- What is the time scale involved and the sequence of events? How much of my time will it take up?
- Get the solicitor to confirm advice and cost in writing.
- Agree a fixed spending limit with your solicitor. If the solicitor is unwilling to explain the costs properly, go elsewhere.

Society, their professional body. The SCB deals with complaints of professional misconduct and poor quality work. It will sometimes direct you to a panel of solicitors to give a second opinion about whether you have a justifiable complaint, and will try to give you a local solicitor who is experienced in these matters. It can order a solicitor to reduce or waive a bill, refund money and correct mistakes. It can award compensation of only up to £1,000.

If you are dissatisfied with the SCB then take your complaint to the Legal Services Ombudsman. He can re-examine the original complaint, and recommend compensation with no maximum limit. If the solicitor fails to pay the recommended compensation, the Ombudsman publishes the details. If you want to sue a solicitor because you feel that you deserve compensation of more than £1,000, then you need to find a solicitor who specialises in this area. This can be more difficult than you would imagine and the Law Society is of little help. You could ask your local CAB or law centre if they can give you a lead. Three solicitors that do specialise in this area are: Ole Hansen, John Wilson and Irwin Mitchell (*see* Addresses).

You can normally sue a solicitor for up to six years after the alleged negligence and longer in limited circumstanes. Your case will be referred to the Solicitors' Indemnity Fund, which operates like any other insurance fund. All solicitors are covered by it as part of their professional practice requirements. Realistically, your case will probably be settled out of court (less than 5 per cent actually get to court) as going to court is costly, in time and money for both parties. An alternative and developing trend is to use Alternative Dispute Resolution Schemes, *see* Conciliation and arbitration, pages 17–18.

Even if you do have a legitimate grievance the system can appear to be constructed to prevent you from getting compensation. Compensation rests upon theorising what would have happened if the mistake had not been made and compensating you for the difference. It does not relate directly to the bill.

The procedures used by the Solicitors' Complaints Bureau have been criticised for favouring solicitors. Complainants are also faced with unacceptable delays and unnecessary bureaucratic barriers.

---

**Tip**

If you intend to sue a solicitor, be careful about going to one who is in the same locality as the solicitor you intend to sue. They may come across each other professionally.

---

The National Consumer Council in a major report in December 1994 went even further. It concluded that the current system for dealing with complaints against solicitors needs wholesale reform and that a new Legal Services Complaints Council – independent from the Law Society – should be set up to replace the SCB. The Legal Services Complaints Council, with a majority of non-solicitors, would deal with complaints of conduct and service. It would combine the role of the SCB and the current Legal Services Ombudsman.

## The future

The Courts and Legal Services Act 1990 has brought about a lot of change in English and Welsh law.

- You have a wider choice of who can represent you in court.
- A lot of cases which were dealt with by the High Court are now dealt with by the county court.
- In some cases you are able to agree that your solicitor will only get paid if he/she wins.
- There are new fixed scales of fees to curb the rising Legal Aid bill.

# USEFUL ADDRESSES

## Conciliation and Arbitration

**Centre for Dispute Resolution**
100 Fetter Lane
London EC4A 1DD
Telephone: 0171 430 1852

**The Chartered Institute of Arbitrators**
Int'l Arbitration Centre
24 Angel Gate
City Road
London EC1V 2RS
Telephone: 0171 837 4483

**National Conciliation Service**
9 North Street
Rugby CV21 2AB
Telephone: 01788 576465

## Legal Aid

**The Council for Licensed Conveyancers**
16 Glebe Road
Chelmsford
Essex CM1 1QG
Telephone: 01245 349599

**The General Council of the Bar**
3 Bedford Row
London WC1R 4DB
Telephone: 0171 242 0082

**The Incorporated Law Society of Ireland**
Blackhall Place
Dublin 7
Telephone: 010 3531 671 0711

**The Law Centres Federation London:**
Duchess House
18-19 Warren Street
London W1P 5DB
Telephone: 0171 387 8570

**Sheffield:**
3rd Floor Arundel Court
177 Arundel Street
Sheffield S1 2NU
Telephone: 0114 2787 0888

**The Law Society of England and Wales**
113 Chancery Lane
London EC2A 1PL
Telephone: 0171 242 1222

**The Law Society of Northern Ireland**
Law Society House
98 Victoria Street
Belfast BT1 3JZ
Telephone: 01232 231614

**The Law Society of Scotland**
26 Drumsheugh Gardens
Edinburgh EH3 7YR
Telephone: 0131 226 7411

**Legal Aid Head Office**
85 Gray's Inn Road
London WC1X 8AA
Telephone: 0171 813 1000

**National Consumer Council**
20 Grosvenor Gardens
London SW1W 0DH
Telephone: 0171 730 3469

**Registry Trust Limited**
173-175 Cleveland Street
London W1P 5PE
Telephone: 0171 380 0133

**The Scottish Legal Aid Board**
44 Drumsheugh Gardens
Edinburgh EH3 7SW
Telephone: 0131 226 7061

**Solicitors' Complaints Bureau**
Victoria Court
8 Dormer Place
Leamington Spa
Warwickshire CV32 5AE
Telephone: 01926 820082

**Victim Support National Office**
Cranmer House
39 Brixton Road
SW9 6DZ
Telephone: 0171 735 9166

## Local Government Ombudsman

*For Greater London, Kent, Surrey, East and West Sussex*
**Local Government Ombudsman**
Mr E Osmotherly
21 Queen Anne's Gate
London SW1H 9BU
Telephone: 0171 915 3210

*For the South-West, the West, the South and most of central England*
**Local Government Ombudsman**
Mr J White
The Oaks, Westwood Way
Westwood Business Park
Coventry CV4 8JB
Telephone: 01203 695999

*For the East Midlands and North of England*

**Local Government Ombudsman**
Mrs P Thomas
Beverley House
17 Shipton Road
York YO3 6FZ
Telephone: 01904 663200

*For Wales*
**The Commission for Local Administration in Wales**
Mr E Moseley
Derwen House, Court Road
Bridgend
Mid Glamorgan CS31 1BN
Telephone: 01656 661325

*For Scotland*
**The Commission for Local Administration in Scotland**
Mr F Marks
23 Walker Street
Edinburgh EH3 7HX
Telephone: 0131 225 5300

**Insurance Ombudsman Bureau**
City Gate One
135 Park Street
London SE1 9EA
Telephone: 0171 928 4488

**The Parliamentary Commissioner of Administration**
Church House
Great Smith Street
London SW1P 3BW
Telephone: 0171 276 2130
(NB He/she handles complaints against central government; complaints must be in writing and referred via an MP.)

## Ombudsmen

**Banking Ombudsman**
Mr L Shurman
70 Gray's Inn Road
London WC1X 8NB
Telephone: 0171 404 9944

**Building Society Ombudsman**
Mr B Murphy
35/37 Grosvenor Gardens
London SW1 X7AW
Telephone: 0171 931 0044

**Corporate Estate Agents' Ombudsman**
Mr D Quayle
Beckett House
4 Bridge Street
Salisbury
Wiltshire SP1 2LX
Telephone: 01722 333306

**Health Service Ombudsman and Parliamentary Ombudsman**
Mr W Reid
Church House
Great Smith Street
London SWP 3BW
Telephone: 0171 276 3000
and 0171 276 2130

**Legal Services Ombudsman**
Mr M Barnes
22 Oxford Court
Oxford Street
Manchester M2 3WQ
Telephone: 0161 236 9532

(NB: The Legal Services Ombudsman reviews handling of complaints against solicitors, barristers and licensed conveyancers. Complaints should first go to the Solicitors Complaints Bureau, the General Council of the Bar or the Council for Licensed Conveyancers.)

**The Pensions Ombudsman**
Dr J Farrand
11 Belgrave Road
London SW1V 1RB
Telephone: 0171 834 9144

## Suing other solicitors

**Ole Hansen**
125 Kennington Road
London SE11 6SF
Telephone: 0171 793 0060

**Irwin Mitchell Solicitors**
Professional Negligence Unit
St Peters House
Hartshead
Sheffield SK1 2EL
Telephone: 0114 276 7777

**Irwin Mitchell Solicitors**
The Citadel
190 Corporation Street
Birmingham B4 6QD
Telephone: 0121 212 1828

**Irwin Mitchell Solicitors**
Friend's Provident House
13-14 South Parade
Leeds LS1 5QS
Telephone: 0113 280 0900

**John Wilson**
Wilsons Solicitors
5 Manor Row
Bradford BD1 4PB
Telephone: 01274 740750

## Tribunals

**Citizens' Charter Publication Line**
Telephone: 0345 223242
(NB: This is not a complaints line but a publications line, which will send you lists of who has charters and a leaflet explaining how you can nominate organisations for the Charter mark, should you so wish!)

**Council on Tribunals**
7th Floor
22 Kingsway
London WC2B 6LE
Telephone: 0171 936 7045

**Lands Tribunal**
48-49 Chancery Lane
London WC2A 1JR
Telephone: 0171 936 7200

**Pension Appeals Tribunal**
48-49 Chancery Lane
London WC2A 1JR
Telephone: 0171 936 7034

**VAT and Duties Tribunals**
15-19 Bedford Avenue
London WC1B 3AS
Telephone: 0171 631 4242

# Chapter 2

# Shopping

What would you be entitled to if your new suit trousers came back from the dry-cleaner a size smaller? What should you do if your mail order goods fail to arrive? Who could help you if a double glazing company refused to repair or refund double glazing that leaked? These types of questions bother us all occasionally – when things go wrong we don't always know who to turn to or what to do.

This chapter details your rights as a consumer and gives practical advice to help you avoid the potential pitfalls of shopping. It starts with the laws that protect the shopper, and then outlines your rights in special situations such as buying on credit, goods under guarantee, mail order sales and second-hand car sales. Every sale and complaint situation involves people as well as rights so the final part of this chapter outlines the best way to approach a complaint situation or letter. You can have a positive influence on the whole process of returning goods if you are polite and know what you are entitled to.

This is the age of customer service and most companies act quickly and fairly to sort out problems. Some even give better conditions than the law requires, like a 14-day money back offer even if you change your mind. However, if a trader is obstructive and you cannot sort out a situation there are organisations and trade associations who can help you. These are detailed at the end of the chapter.

## THE LAWS THAT PROTECT YOU

### Sale of Goods Act

This law applies when you buy from retailers as an ordinary customer. It ensures that goods:

- are of satisfactory quality (free from any defects). For example, if you buy a clothes pattern all the pattern pieces should meet up.

- are fit for the purpose for which they are intended, including any purpose mentioned to the seller. If you say that you are looking for windscreen wiper blades for a 1983 Renault 5 the seller must sell you something that fits.
- correspond with their description. If an item is described as leather it must be leather. The law also states that the bulk of the goods will correspond with the sample – for example, if you order a fitted kitchen on the basis of a sample door, all the doors should be of the same quality when they arrive.

## Misrepresentation Act 1967

It is illegal to make false statements about goods. Even if a seller is acting innocently or to the best of his knowledge, he is responsible if his description is a distortion, falsification or exaggeration of the truth.

## Trade Descriptions Act 1968

Whenever goods or services are for sale, anything relevant that is said about them in writing or verbally is a trade description. Trade descriptions must not be false. Even if sellers are acting innocently, and to the best of their knowledge, they are responsible if their representation is untrue. Trading Standards Departments can also take action against anyone who gives a false description of the goods or services they provide. For example, coats described as 'waterproof' must not let in the rain.

## Consumer Protection Act 1987, part I

Where any damage is caused wholly or partly by a defect in a product, the producer will be liable for the damage and so will anyone who has held him or herself out to be the producer by putting their name on the product or packaging, or anyone who imports it from outside the EC into one of the member states.

- Injured parties must bring a claim for the damage within three years of the date when the cause of action occurred. Only one claim can be made for damages. Lawyers sometimes advise injured parties to wait before claiming (but no longer than three years) so that the full effects of any injuries are known; for example, whiplash may lead to migraines and backache. Wait and see.

- Damages over £275 are claimed from the producer under these laws. Smaller amounts may be claimed from the retailer under the laws of negligence.

### Consumer Protection Act 1987, parts II & III
This makes it a criminal offence to supply unsafe goods. Part II protects consumers from over-charging and false price comparisons.

### Laws of negligence
Where there is a duty of care and it is breached you may have a case against the responsible party. For example, a manufacturer is expected to exercise reasonable care in ensuring the safety of his product. It is up to the consumer to prove that the manufacturer has been at fault in incidents where the product has caused material damage or personal injury. Negligence law applies to a full range of manufactured products, from hair dyes to cars, and also to services. Statements restricting liability – for example, a notice in a multi-storey car park saying that the owner accepts no responsibility for damage to property – may not be held as reasonable in a court of law.

### Supply of Goods and Services Act 1982
The consumer can expect 'a reasonable standard' of workmanship in a contract for work or materials. The loose phrasing of this law allows considerable room for dispute as to what is reasonable and what is not.

### Unsolicited Goods and Services Act 1971
After six months' unsolicited goods can be used, dealt with or disposed of as if they were unconditional gifts. However, you must either keep them for six months so that the sender can come and collect them, or write to the sender, stating that the goods were unsolicited and giving the address from which the sender should collect them. If they are not collected within 30 days they become yours.

### Weights and Measures Act 1985

Traders must sell full measures. Trading Standards Officers frequently check garages and pubs to see that this law is upheld.

All weighing and measuring equipment must be accurate. Pre-packaged goods should show a weight and price. All loose goods should be sold over a weighing machine except a few that can be sold by number.

### Arbitration Agreements Act 1988

*See* Arbitration, page 17.

### Price Marking Order 1991

This law requires price displays to be shown on most goods.

### Food Safety Act 1990

It is an offence to sell food which is:
- unfit for human consumption
- injurious to health
- contaminated to the extent that it cannot reasonably be used for human consumption

A misleading description of the nature, quality and substance of food is also an offence. Misdescription or any other criminal offence outlined above applies even if a sale does not take place.

## TRADE ASSOCIATIONS AND CODES OF PRACTICE

Traders often belong to trade associations, which work to maintain high standards within an industry. Some have codes of practice, and some run low-cost conciliation or arbitration schemes to sort out problems between their members and customers.

ABTA, the Association of British Travel Agents, is a well-known trade association which protects consumers. If you book a holiday with an ABTA member you can be sure that all your money will be refunded if the travel agent goes out of business. Similar associations operate to protect your shopping rights.

Codes of practice are voluntary and do not have the power of legislation. However, it is in the interests of all members to see that codes of practice are upheld, and if traders do break codes, an outside arbitrator should find in your favour.

Trade associations can be particularly useful when you are buying services (*see* Chapter 3, Services).

Trade associations exist for anything from mail order (*see* Buying goods by post and mail order, page 37) to electrical retailers. Useful contact numbers are listed at the end of the chapter. It is always worth checking that a trader is a member of the bodies that he claims.

## SPECIAL CASES

When you buy goods, a 'contract' is made between you and the seller. The rights that come with that contract vary depending on what you buy, how you pay for it, and from whom you buy it.

### Shops and the right to say 'No'

It is a popular misconception that shopkeepers are obliged to sell anything they have on display. They are not. Goods displayed in shops are 'an invitation to treat', and a shopkeeper is not obliged to accept your offer to buy. You may be absolutely desperate for the last paper lampshade in the shop but if the seller does not want to sell it – because it's on display, for example – he does not have to. However, once your offer has been accepted the deal is on, and neither the shopkeeper nor the customer can back out. If goods are faulty then you are entitled to a refund if you return them within a reasonable time (*see* Acceptance, page 47).

### Buying on credit

Normally if something goes wrong with a product you've bought, you go back to the seller, and if the seller won't help or has gone bust then you've got problems. Buying on credit, however, gives you some extra rights. If you pay over £100 for the goods the lender also becomes equally liable for anything which goes wrong so you can make a claim against them.

---

> ### Different kinds of plastic
>
> Debit cards are like plastic cheques. They withdraw the money straight from your account. Charge cards allow you to put off paying for goods till the end of the month – but they do not let you spread the cost over an indefinite period in return for interest payments.

Special rules apply to goods bought on credit at home (ie not in a shop or other trade premises). Although the contract is made when the seller agrees to sell the goods, customers usually have five days in which they can change their mind and cancel the contract.

**Cancelling credit** Under certain circumstances it is possible to cancel a credit deal. Check your cancellation rights *before* you sign, and act quickly if you do change your mind. Time limits are tight. You should be able to cancel if:

- you signed the agreement at home rather than in a shop or on the lender's or supplier's premises
- you made the deal within the last few days
- you talked to the lender in person rather than on the phone

### Buying goods by post and mail order

When you buy by post the contract is made when the seller posts an acceptance letter, confirmation, receipt, or the goods themselves. Even if you have not received the letter or it is lost in the post, the contract still stands. If you do cancel, the seller should promptly refund the purchase price or deposit. Sale of Goods Act rights are the same when buying from home by mail order as when buying from a shop.

A number of mail order trade associations exist. While their codes of

---

> ### Repayment hassles
>
> If you run into problems with repayments, speak to the lender about it – don't sit back and do nothing.

---

### Fools' gold

Credit is readily available and can also be falsely alluring. Before you buy on credit consider:

- the total cost of the loan – can you really afford to pay it back?
- other credit offers – can you get the loan cheaper elsewhere? The annual percentage rate of charge (APR) is generally the best indicator: the lower the APR the better the deal. However 0 per cent APR and other bargain deals may have hidden costs. The Office of Fair Trading produces a leaflet called 'Credit wise – a guide to trouble-free credit' (see end of chapter for address). Be wary of LOAN SHARKS who charge high rates of interest.
- other ways of financing the purchase – do you need to use credit?
- all the small print – do not sign until you have read it in full and asked the trader to explain any clauses you are unsure of. If you sign a contract agreeing to the payments, it is likely to be legally binding.

---

practice are not legally binding, the organisation and its members undertake to uphold them. Look out for their symbols.

## Tips on postal buying

- Never send cash through the post. Use a cheque or postal order and keep the stub or counterfoil as proof of purchase.
- If you are replying to an advert in a newspaper or magazine keep it, together with the name of the magazine. If the goods don't arrive you'll need it.
- Read the rules. If the goods are faulty you should not have to pay for return postage – but some companies insist that you do. Also, can the company increase the price of the goods?
- Look for a MOPS sign when answering adverts, or MOTA when buying from a catalogue.
- Goods should be delivered within a reasonable time. Check how long the company allows for delivery. If the goods do not arrive within this time you can ask for a refund, or set a new date by which you want to receive the goods.

- If possible check the goods on arrival. If you cannot, write 'not examined' on the delivery note so that it is clear that you have not checked or accepted them yet.
- If goods are faulty return them immediately, with a note explaining the fault. Sending by registered or recorded post is advisable. You can phone to tell the company that you are returning the goods and why.
- Most companies give you the right to inspect the goods and return them within a certain number of days if you change your mind.

## Protection schemes

- MOPS – Mail Order Protection Scheme

Newspapers and magazines that run MOPS ensure that their readers will not lose money if the advertiser stops trading. (It does not apply to classified small-ads or ads for perishable foods or medical products.)

- MOTA – Mail Order Traders' Association

The MOTA scheme is run for mail-order catalogues. MOTA send goods 'on approval', giving you a specified time (14 days plus) to return them.

## Book and record clubs

How many books/records will you have to buy? Do inflated prices or postage and package charges make the deal expensive? It's worth asking what types of books/records are on normal lists and looking at past lists – people have been taken in by attractive ranges at Christmas.

## Signed contracts and deposits

If you put down a deposit for a car, you are doing more than reserving it, you are promising to buy it. Under section 49 of the Sale of Goods Act, where goods have been ordered and the consumer wrongfully refuses to

---

### Piles of junk mail

The direct marketing boom has left mountains of paper offering goods and services on many doorsteps. If you want your name deleted from direct mailing lists contact the Mailing Preference Service (*see* page 53).

accept them (ie without a valid reason for rejection) and pay, the retailer can sue for the price of the goods and damages. A signed contract where no deposit has been paid is as legally binding as a signed contract and a deposit.

Sellers of goods such as made-to-measure furniture or holidays often ask you to provide a deposit 'as a sign of good faith'. It is up to you whether to accept such a contract, but once you have you must pay up. *Do not pay in advance unless you have to; if the firm goes out of business you could get little or nothing back.*

## Ordering goods

If you have to order something, it is best to agree a date by which you want it. It is not unheard of for people to wait for over a year for curtains to match their sofas. If you agree a delivery time you can refuse to accept the goods if they are late. It is also advisable to agree a fixed price and any delivery costs. Get the agreement in writing where possible.

## Waiting for a delivery

Sometimes customers order an item and are then told it is out of stock and cannot be supplied for some time. Can they back out of the transaction and take their custom to another shop that can offer immediate delivery? Generally the answer will be no, for there is already a binding contract with the shopkeeper – unless, of course, it was specifically agreed that the goods should be ready by a particular date, or the customer has made time 'of the essence'.

Once a contract has been made and a price agreed, the trader cannot ask you to pay more than the price you saw when you placed your order. (A change in VAT can, however, be passed on.) But when ordering from a catalogue or brochure which says something open-ended like 'subject to price fluctuations' or 'prices correct at the time of going to print', the customer may have to pay the new current price.

Sometimes you are asked to sign for goods when they are delivered. There is no reason to refuse, as long as the signature is no more than proof of delivery. Not so if it is a satisfaction note stating that the goods are satisfactory or in good order. Unless there is a chance to look at them properly first, it is better to write 'goods not examined'.

## Guarantees

A manufacturer's guarantee is in addition to, not instead of, your normal rights. Make sure that the retailer fills in the guarantee card, and then send it off if required. Goods that are faulty should be returned to the shop you bought them from, even if they are under guarantee by the manufacturer. Guarantees are useful because they indicate the minimum period (usually a year) that the item must be operable for.

## Extended guarantees

Goods such as TVs and dishwashers sometimes offer extended guarantees or warranties. You normally have to pay extra for them. Read the details of the cover carefully, noting exclusions.

## Second-hand goods

Second-hand goods bought from a trader are covered by the Sale of Goods Act; you have the same rights but a lower standard is applied – second-hand goods cannot be expected to be of the same quality as new ones.

Although your legal rights are similar, the practicalities are very different. The mercurial nature of traders and market stalls makes it easier for unscrupulous traders to side-step legislation.

There are additional problems in buying second-hand goods: they may have been manufactured before the safety legislation. Common problems

---

### Collecting proof

If you buy something on the basis of what the seller says, then you may be able to claim damages.

- Take a witness.
- Ask for a written description of the goods.
- Keep any private ads you buy from – wording such as 'good condition' may help you later.

reported by Trading Standards Officers include old toys that contravene safety laws, second-hand sofas that contain potentially lethal foam, and used tyres that are faulty. Privately bought goods *do* have to be as described but they do not have to be free of faults. The rule is 'buyer beware', so check what you are getting before you buy.

It is a criminal offence for trade sellers to masquerade as private sellers (using small-ads and giving only their private addresses), in order to get away with selling goods that are of a lower standard, or defective. They must make some positive indication they are selling in the course of trade or business (for example, using the word 'Trade' at the end of the advert).

## Buying a car privately

The rules on satisfactory quality and fitness for purpose do not apply to private car sales. If you by a car privately it need only be 'as described' by the seller and roadworthy (as defined by the Road Traffic Act). Therefore, to protect yourself, take the following precautions:

- make sure that the seller's name is correct and that they live at the address they give you (directory enquiries and the electoral register are useful sources). You may need to track them down later.
- Inspect the vehicle registration document, MOT certificate and servicing history *before* you sign the deal. Beware of clocking – the illegal practice of lowering the mileage on the clock.
- Look in a used car guide to check that the price you are paying is fair.
- If you are dubious about the seller, and think that they might actually be a dealer posing as a private individual, contact your local Trading Standards Officers. They may be able to confirm your suspicions.
- Take an expert with you if you can. If you are paying a lot for the car it may be worth having a garage, the AA or the RAC inspect it for you. Note that while the AA and RAC will give you a report on the car, they will not be held to it – if something goes wrong you cannot sue them for misinformation.
- Ask questions and make a note of the seller's claims. A witness can be invaluable.

> **Tip:**
> Check the other adverts in the newspaper or magazine to see if a phone
> number occurs more than once.

### Car boot sales

Car boot sales now attract a large number of traders and organised sellers
as well as Joe Public and the content of his attic. Some traders may be
reputable but there are a number of cowboys on the circuit selling goods
that do not meet legal requirements. When you buy, take a note of the
seller's vehicle type, colour and registration number as well as their name
and address. This will increase your chances of justice if there is a problem
at a later date. Be particularly aware of

- **Unsafe electrical appliances** Check electrical appliances thoroughly
  before plugging them in. Wrongly wired plugs, incorrect fuses, worn
  flex and accessibility to live parts can all be assessed visually. Trading
  Standards Officers warn that the dangers are very real – one man was
  electrocuted while using a second-hand sander bought at a car boot sale.
- **Counterfeit goods** Counterfeit video tapes, perfumes and trainers are
  often on sale. They might look like bargains but will they work and
  are they worth it? Do you really want a 'designer' perfume? One
  group of Trading Standards Officers seized counterfeit perfumes
  containing nothing less than pond water.
- **Stolen goods** It is impossible to tell whether goods are stolen –
  though new/good products at bargain prices and obscured
  identification marks are clues.
- **Unsafe toys** It is unlikely that old toys will comply with current safety
  legislation – check for detachable parts and spikes.
- **Out-of-date food** Look for sell-by dates on food and don't buy it if
  they are not shown.

### Doorstep and 'Party Plan' purchases

Doorstep purchases and goods bought at organised selling parties at
someone's home (Tupperware parties, for example) are covered by the
same laws as goods bought in shops; they must be of satisfactory quality,

---

### Sugging

'Sugging', selling under the guise of doing something else, is a popular ruse. Sellers will kid you into completing a survey, answering a prize draw, or turning up to claim a free trial of an incentive like a satellite dish – and then they will try to sell to you. Be wary.

---

fit for their purpose and 'as described'. However, these legal rights are not much use if you cannot find the doorstep seller or party plan organisers.

- Make sure that you get a receipt.
- Ask callers/party organisers for their full names, find out whom they represent, and keep a note of the firm's address.

- Do not sign anything without first reading it carefully. If you do not understand it fully, do not sign at all.
- Don't be pressurised into buying. Doorstep and party plan sellers are masters of psychology, offering special discounts, free gifts and other incentives if you agree to sign immediately. You are being manipulated – so don't buy unless you are sure.

### Auctions

Auctioneers, unlike traders, can refuse to accept responsibility for the quality of the goods they sell. Typically the conditions of sale (detailed in auction catalogues) deny responsibility for work. Read the exclusion clauses before the hammer has fallen – afterwards it will be too late to back out. The auction house, Christie's, writes, 'None of the sellers, Christie's, its employers or agents is responsible for the correctness of any statement as to the authorship, origin, date, age, size, medium, attribution or provenance of any lot, for any other errors of description or for any faults or defects of the lot.' The strength of this claim was tested in court for the first time in 1994, when a £500,000 painting described as 'by Schiele' turned out to be a fake. The judge ruled that a buyer has the right of return/money back in cases of forgery or deceit only. Otherwise a buyer 'must satisfy himself over the goods and cannot rely upon what the auctioneers have said'.

---

### Subtle distinctions

- 'Raspberry flavoured' products must get their flavour from real rasperries
- 'Raspberry flavour' products mimic the taste of raspberry but don't have to have anything to do with the real thing
- Check the alcohol level of 'low-alcohol' booze. Criteria vary: 'low' could mean virtually 'no'.

### Food and restaurants

Some of the requirements of the Food Safety Act 1990 overlap with other legislation. For example, it is an offence to have a false or misleading description of the nature, quality or substance of food and an offence if the nature, quality or substance of food is not of the standard demanded. It is an offence to supply food which is :

- unfit for human consumption
- injurious to health
- contaminated to the extent that it cannot reasonably be used for human consumption.

The Environmental Health Department of each local authority also enforces certain laws that cover public health matters, such as inspecting places where food is stored, prepared and sold, and also cleanliness in other establishments used by consumers, such as hairdressing and beauty salons. In the London boroughs the division of work between Environmental Health Departments and Trading Standards varies.

## TAKING ACTION IF THINGS GO WRONG

You are entitled to a refund on faulty goods as long as you return them within a reasonable time. The value of the refund will depend on how long you have had the item. You may be offered a replacement or free repair but you do not have to agree to it – you can insist on your money back.

If you do accept a repair or replacement then you may not be able to ask for your money back if something else goes wrong at a later date. If you do not want to be caught in a cycle of repairs, make an agreement

---

**Credit notes**

- Credit notes are not a remedy recognised by the law and are therefore either less or more than you are entitled to. They should only be accepted if you have no legal rights.
- Once you have accepted a credit note you cannot demand that it be exchanged for cash.
- Some credit notes have time limits attached to them.

---

with the shopkeeper – in writing if possible – that if anything else goes wrong you will want a refund.

### Are you sure you're in the right?
Before you return something you've bought, stop and consider your position. Should you have spotted the fault when you inspected the goods? Are you expecting a lot from a cheap and cheerful product? Were you told about the fault? Have you really just changed your mind? Did you make a mistake? If you answered 'yes' to any of these questions, you do not have a case. If you answered no, *see* What to do with faulty goods, page 47.

### Examining before you buy
Defects which are specifically drawn to buyers' attention before they actually buy are excepted, and so are defects which they ought to have discovered if they had examined the goods before buying.

### Changing your mind
Legally you are only entitled to a refund if goods are faulty *and* you bought them; but many shops allow you to exchange a good if you change your mind or if you've received it as a gift. GHI rang 13 high street stores and all but two offered an exchange or vouchers. John Lewis and Freeman Hardy & Willis said that they might offer a cash refund.

If you are unsure about a purchase, for example, if you are buying for someone and you don't know what size they take, you can ask whether you can exchange or refund. If they say yes, and it is not store policy to give refunds, make sure you get it in writing so that you will be able to take the goods back.

## What to do with faulty goods
- Stop using the item immediately.
- Return to the seller as soon as possible. If you cannot take it back quickly, phone the seller.
- If you continue to use the goods or delay in returning them the seller may argue that you have legally 'accepted' the goods.
- You do not have to return faulty goods at your own expense – it is the shop, for example, that should pay for the return of a faulty dishwasher.

## Acceptance
If you keep goods beyond *a reasonable time* or continue to use them, the law says that you have 'accepted' them and are therefore not entitled to a refund. What is considered reasonable depends on the goods and the circumstances. Keeping shoes for a few weeks after they have broken can be argued as constituting acceptance, whereas keeping a mower for eight months before using it and finding it is faulty is not. The safest approach is to reject faulty goods as soon as possible after purchase.

Faults must be found and reported to the shop within a 'reasonable time' in order for you to be entitled to a refund. It is tempting to persuade oneself that paying extra for high quality goods – the 'best on the market' – will mean they will 'last forever', but the law does not make allowance for this type of shopper's expectations. Faults found within a few weeks will probably be refunded but after that you take your chances. Any faults found after a year has elapsed will only be replaced/refunded on account of manufacturer's/shop's goodwill or guarantee.

## How to complain
When you get to the shop there are ways of making the complaint process less painful. Bear the following in mind:

- Remain calm and polite at all times.
- Stick to the matter at hand. Avoid getting side-tracked by irrelevancies, no matter how annoying and frustrating they may be. You may have been sent from department to department, been insulted by shop assistants, or been severely inconvenienced by the goods that are faulty, but are any of these frustrations strictly relevant to the solution of your complaint?
- You must have proof of purchase to make a successful claim so always keep your receipts or other proof of purchase (sales tag, cheque stub, debit or credit card or charge card receipt, or witness). Stores will accept responsibility for problems with own-brand goods but will often give replacements or credit vouchers rather than refunds.
- Keep a record of dates and details of complaints (when the fault appeared, whom you spoke to about it, etc) and put your complaint into writing if it is not successful at first.

### Heard this one before?

While most companies have adopted good customer service policies, some will still give you the run-around. Consumers often face the following stock answers to their complaints:

**'No one else has complained'** This was the comment when a swimming costume (one actually designed for competitive swimming) leaked dye on to towels every time it was wet.
**Your response:** You are complaining about your item only. It is faulty and therefore, by law, you are entitled to a refund. Other people's attitudes are not relevant to your goods.

**'Take the matter up with the manufacturer'** This comes most often from sellers of electrical goods, especially those under guarantee.
**Your response:** Your contract is with the seller and not the manufacturer, and it is therefore the seller's responsibility to sort it out.

---

### Proof of purchase

To return faulty goods, proof of purchase is required. This can take a variety of forms:

- a garment tag with the company name
- a witness to the purchase
- a cheque stub
- a credit card receipt
- a receipt

---

**'Sales goods cannot be returned'** You have the same rights when you buy sales goods as at any other time. Shops' goodwill policies (where they allow you to return goods when you have changed your mind, for example) may change, but your statutory rights remain.

**'Not without a receipt'** Legally, all you need is proof of purchase. Stick to the facts and the relevant points of law and keep calm and you should reach a solution quickly. If you are not getting a satisfactory response, appeal to a higher authority.

## Faulty goods liable for damages or injury

The Consumer Protection Act of 1987 states that where any damage is caused wholly or partly by a defect in a product, the producer will be liable for the damage and so will anyone who has held him or herself out to be the producer by putting their name on the product or its packaging.

'Damage' means death, personal injury or any loss of or damage to any private property caused by defective goods. 'Defective' does not mean 'unfit' or 'unsatisfactory' in the Sale of Goods Act sense, but unsafe or dangerous. The following are examples of this damage caused by defective goods:

- An electrical appliance that overheats, causing a fire.
- A bottle that explodes because the glass cannot stand the pressure created by the contents, causing cuts to persons standing nearby.

- Unguarded moving parts of a child's carriage that have allowed a baby to put its fingers into contact with sharp cogs.

Liability for an unsafe product remains with anyone who imports it from outside the EC into one of the member states in the course of business.

**Time for claiming** The injured party must bring a claim within three years of the date when the cause of the action occurred. Where the Consumer Protection Act does not apply (under £275 damages or out of time), the consumer would have to invoke the laws of negligence and contract to try and get redress.

**Taking it further** Give the offender a reasonable time to sort the problem out but if you don't reach a satisfactory solution take it further. The Citizens' Advice Bureau or local Trading Standards Department should be able to help. Another step is to see if there is a trade association that can help.

### Trade associations and regulatory bodies

They have their own conciliation or arbitration schemes for resolving disputes between traders and consumers. Such schemes tend to be informal and inexpensive. Conciliation (*see*, page 18) aims to help the parties resolve the problems themselves but the resolution is not legally binding. If you are not satisfied you can move on to arbitration or court.

**Public utilities** Some public utilities (even some of the now-privatised ones), such as gas, electricity, telephones, the post office, the railway, have a consumer or consultative council or a users' committee to help sort out problems. The local contact point and brief instructions are usually on the back of the current bill (*see* Chapter 3).

**Banks and building societies** These have official ombudsmen (regulators). For more about them *see* Ombudsmen, page 19.

### Arbitration

This is cheap and straightforward. Both parties submit their cases, and an independent arbitrator decides the rights and wrongs of the case, and the level of damages.

- The arbitrator that hears a case is usually an expert in the field, appointed by the Chartered Institute of Arbitrators.
- A smallish fee is payable.
- Arbitration can take place only if both parties agree.

### Going to court

Going to court should be a last resort, and is generally the exception. There are less drastic routes for settling disputes. Court action and how to take it are discussed in Chapter 1.

# WHO CAN HELP

### Useful organisations

### Citizens' Advice Bureaux (CABx)

These offer free advice, information and assistance with consumer problems. The number of your local one can be found in the phone book.

### Environmental Health Departments

These protect public health. They have powers to inspect the cleanliness of places where food is stored, prepared and sold, and also of other establishments used by consumers, such as hairdressers and beauty salons. They should be contacted if a shop sells mouldy food, if you think you contracted food poisoning from a venue, or if objects such as glass are found in your food. They are part of local authorities.

### Trading Standards Departments

These departments investigate cases involving unfair trading, false descriptions, product safety, metrology (the accuracy of measures such as petrol pumps and pub spirits), and consumer credit. Where there is an offence it is the Trading Standards Officer who investigates. Many departments are not funded to deal with individual civil complaints but can give general advice.

Where there is an offence, it is the Trading Standards Officer who prosecutes if necessary. The main aim is to put things right so there may be a warning instead of a prosecution.

A complaint to a Trading Standards Office can be made on the telephone, in writing, in person, by letter or by fax. If the citizen's complaint should lead to a prosecution, he or she may be asked for a witness statement but it is uncommon to have to go to the magistrates' court or the Crown Court as a witness.

Contact your local Trading Standards Office via the local council office or town hall.

**Office of Fair Trading**
Public Liaison Unit
Field House
15-25 Bream's Buildings
London EC4A 1PR
OFT Public Liaison Line: 01345 224499

The OFT protects consumers by encouraging competition among businesses and making sure that trading practices are as fair as possible. The Public Liaison Unit will give advice on where to turn for assistance with a particular problem, but cannot intervene to help with individual disputes. They can, however, advise you of the official, voluntary and trade organisations who may be able to intervene.

The Office of Fair Trading leaflet *Creditwise* (and other consumer leaflets) are available from:

**The Office of Fair Trading**
PO Box 2
Central Way
Feltham
Middlesex TW14 0TG
0181 398 3405

# USEFUL ADDRESSES

**Automobile Association (AA)**
Technical Information Unit
Lambert House
Stockport Road
Cheadle
Cheshire SK8 2DY

**Consumers' Association**
2 Marylebone Road
London NW1 4DX
(NB: Campaigns actively for
improvements in goods and
services, in both the public
and private sector. Provides an
advisory service for its
members, although it cannot
offer assistance to other
individuals with problems.)

**Direct Marketing Association**
Haymarket House
1 Oxendon Street
London SW1Y 4EE
Telephone: 0171 321 2525

**Direct Selling Association
Limited**
29 Floral Street
London WC2E 9DP
Telephone: 0171 497 1234

**Glass and Glazing Federation**
44-48 Borough High Street
London SE1 1XB
Telephone: 0171 403 7177

**HPI Autodata**
Dolphin House
PO Box 61
New Street
Salisbury
Wiltshire SP1 2TB
Telephone: 01722 422422

**Mail Order Traders'
Association**
100 Old Hall Street
Liverpool L3 9TD
Telephone: 0151 227 4181

**Mailing Preference Service**
Freepost 22
London W1E 7EZ
Telephone: 0171 738 1625

**National Federation of
Consumer Groups (NFCG)**
12 Mosley Street
Newcastle upon Tyne
NE1 1DE
(NB: Will be able to give you
the address of your local
group, which raises issues of
concern in your area, and
presses for improvements
where necessary.)

**National Newspapers' Mail
Order Protection Scheme Ltd**
16 Tooks Court
London EC4A 1LB
Telephone: 0171 405 6806
(NB: Contact the complaints
section of the paper concerned
first. If you have no success,
you can contact MOPS Head
Office.)

**Qualitas National
Conciliation Service**
Chief Conciliation Officer
30 Harcourt Street
London W1H 2AA
Telephone: 0171 706 2458

**The Radio, Electrical and
Television Retailers'
Association Limited**
RETRA House
1 Ampthill Street
Bedford MK42 9EY
Telephone: 01234 269110

**Royal Automobile Club
(RAC)**
PO Box 100
RAC House
Bartlett Street
South Croydon
Surrey CR2 6XW
Telephone: 0181 686 0088

**SATRA**
Satra House
Rockingham Road
Kettering
Northants NN16 9JH
Telephone: 01536 410000

# Chapter 3

# Services

When buying services, be it a haircut, dry-cleaning or having building work carried out, you are entitled to certain standards. In many respects your legal position is similar to when you buy goods. It is a question of contract. According to the Supply of Goods and Services Act 1994, three basic rules apply. A job must be carried out with:

### 'Reasonable care and skill'

A job should be done to a proper standard of workmanship. While the heart of the law is clear, 'reasonable care and skill' is a phrase that is open to interpretation, and notoriously difficult to apply. If you do have problems with a service, another firm in the same business, of good repute, is best qualified to offer a professional opinion about the standard of work undertaken. Unfortunately, this will be at your expense. A written quote for remedying the faults from the second firm will indicate how large the damages claim should be.

### 'Reasonable time'

A builder shouldn't take five years to repair your roof, so set a completion date with the firm when you ask them to undertake the work. If work is not carried out within a reasonable time you can claim for damages, inconvenience, or the cost of getting another firm to complete it.

### 'Reasonable cost'

According to the law, work undertaken should be done 'at a reasonable cost'. To avoid problems, always obtain an estimate or quote in advance. If a price is fixed at the outset you cannot complain later that it is unreasonable. Always obtain more than one quote for comparison.

Sometimes jobs, such as fitting a new exhaust, involve both goods (the exhaust) and services (fitting). The goods are covered by law in the same

---

### Quote and Estimates

A fixed price or **quote** is binding on the parties, even if the job should turn out to involve considerably more, or less, work than was originally envisaged. When accepting it is worth adding that you accept their fixed quotation.

With **estimates**, the position is less clear-cut. If the eventual bill is higher than the original estimate, you will have to pay the increased amount – assuming, of course, that it is a 'reasonable' price for the work done.

It is advisable to stipulate, where appropriate, that 'extra work shall be carried out only on my written instructions'.

When accepting any estimate or quotation check how long it is valid for.

---

way as if you buy them directly; they must be of satisfactory quality and fit for the purpose for which they are intended.

## HOW TO GET GOOD SERVICE

- Get full written details of the job to be carried out.
- Obtain three written quotations for the work – itemising each part of it. This can stop 'hidden extras' being found along the way.
- Choose companies that are members of recognised trade associations.
- Read a contract – does it state that the firm can increase the price of a job halfway through?
- Never pay the full sum in advance. It is usual for service providers to ask for deposits and part payments to cover the cost of their materials. Pay if you are happy with the job.
- Get receipts for every payment that you make – dated, with the trader's name and address written clearly.
- Make it clear that firms can only undertake extra work with your agreement at the outset. You do not have to pay for something that you did not agree at the beginning.
- Always get guarantees for the work carried out.

## WHAT TO DO ABOUT BAD SERVICE

If you are unhappy with a service it can be more difficult to sort out than a faulty product. You must decide how much of the work is unsatisfactory. What value is attached to that part of the work? Was it reasonable for the service provider to work for so many hours on that job? How much will it cost to put the error right?

If the business or person providing the service is a member of a trade association, then it may be easier to get things put right, otherwise you will have to go to an independent arbitrator. Most members of trade associations have codes of practice to adhere to. Some offer conciliation should problems arise.

If you don't agree with the bill, pay what you think is reasonable, giving your reasons. This puts the ball in his court – he can take further action if he wants. If you have to pay up to get your car back or scaffolding removed then write '**without prejudice**' on the bill so that you can take it up later.

Don't sign a **satisfaction note** until you are sure that you are satisfied, or write 'not tested yet' on it.

## HOME IMPROVEMENTS AND REPAIRS

If anything goes wrong with your home your first reaction is probably to grab the phone and dial the first number you come across in the Yellow Pages. Try not to panic, however – think first, not later. It's worth spending extra having proper advice and surveys rather than cutting financial corners or using the first plumber/builder/decorator who's available. Anyone can set themselves up in these fields: they don't need to have any recognised qualification or apprenticeship.

### The contract

When you have chosen a company, drawing up an airtight contract is the next stage. This should include:

- a breakdown of the work to be carried out, itemising costs.

### Avoiding cowboy workmanship

- If possible ask friends and neighbours for recommendations of good companies – word of mouth is the best guarantee.
- Always get several quotes which are professionally presented and include their terms and conditions. Obtain advice from architects and surveyors for large jobs.
- Expect a professional manner at all times even when they answer the phone.
- Service people should always be easy to contact – mobile phones and pagers are a must.
- Don't put up with late starts.
- Workers should look presentable.
- The job should be fully explained to you throughout.
- Workers should tidy up at the end of each day.
- They should work around you – not the other way round.
- Look for professional qualifications and membership of reputable trade bodies who have codes of practice. It's worth checking with the trade association that they are still members before you employ them.

- a statement saying that the estimate or quotation must not be exceeded without your permission. If you are not consulted then he should pay.
- a statement saying that only materials of satisfactory quality will be used.
- start and completion dates. If you need the work to be finished by a particular date you can specify this in the contract. If it is not completed within that time, you have the right to cancel and claim back any advance payment. Be fair and realistic here – bad weather, for example, may have played a part.
- cancellation rights. This will give you a few days' leeway if you change your mind after signing the contract although agreements signed on trade premises are not normally cancellable.
- guarantees for finished work. Be warned though: long-term guarantees are useless if the firm goes out of business unless they are insurance backed.

- who is responsible for repair work to any damaged areas. For example, if double glazing is installed should they patch up surrounding decor if damaged?
- who will clear up after the work is completed.
- liability if serious damage is caused – there should not be an upper limit here.

The company should inform you if they are going to subcontract any of the work. If they are, ensure that they admit full liability for the subcontractors' work.

The contract should be typed and signed by both parties.

If they will not agree to put anything in writing, go elsewhere. Alternatively, if you are required to sign their contract, add any extra clauses from above which are not included and delete anything you disagree with. Read the small print.

You are the employer so the contract must be your terms and conditions.

The tighter the contract, the easier it will be to sort out any disagreement. Should there be a problem you can decide to:

- only pay what you feel is owing
- demand that the work be redone to the satisfactory standard
- find another company to complete the work if they exceed the price quoted and only pay for the work done; or, if they have finished, only pay the amount stated in the quote.

### Builders

Typical problems are poor workmanship and problems due to subcontracting the work.

To protect yourself from cowboys look out for companies who are members of the Chartered Institute of Building and so are professionally qualified to carry out building works. This means that their executives or partners have carried out a series of exams to degree level, including a Professional Interview and have relevant professional experience.

The CIOB is independent and self-regulating but is not a trade association.

## Architects, surveyors and structural engineers

These are classed as professionals so look for membership of professional institutes such as the Royal Institute of British Architects, Royal Institution of Chartered Surveyors or Institution of Structural Engineers. This means they have certain qualifications and must adhere to their Institute's code of conduct. Look for the letters ARICS or FRICS after their name. Architects must also be registered by law with the Architects Registration Council of UK.

Professional bodies such as these really only help the individual in cases of misconduct – they stress they are not a public advisory service or legal advice bureau. However, they are there to keep up standards and can suggest other members to act as arbitrators or conciliators in disputes between members and clients.

When choosing a chartered surveyor, it's worth going for a local firm because they are more likely to know what is going on in your area regarding any land peculiarities, Council plans, etc. Check that they have indemnity insurance.

## Plumbing and heating

Plumbers are generally called for in emergencies, leaving us wide open to exploitation. If you have problems with blocked drains it's worth contacting your local authority Environmental Health Department to check whose responsibility it is.

The Institute of Plumbing has developed its own Code of Professional Standards, their 'key to quality'. All 13,000 members have signed up to the Code and risk suspension if they break it. (Unfortunately, this would not prevent them from working.)

The Institute produces an annual directory containing details of registered plumbers and companies. This is available from libraries, Citizens' Advice Bureaux, Trading Standards Departments, etc. You will also find registered plumbers in the Yellow Pages and local directories.

If you have a complaint against a member contact the Institute. Serious complaints will be

> **Tip**
> Pay only for materials in advance and ask for receipts.

---

### How to complain about a survey

If you've had a house surveyed and feel the surveyor missed serious defects you must get a second opinion from another surveyor as soon as possible. This means, of course, paying out another £500 plus if it is a full building survey but you can sue if the original surveyor is found to be negligent. The second survey must show that the first should have outlined the fault and that you have lost money (ie spent more than necessary on the new house).

You can go either to court or to an arbitrator. If you go to court the law says that you can only claim back the difference in value between the price you paid for the house and what you would have paid had you known about the problem. In reality you might have preferred to withdraw your offer.

---

referred to the Institute's Membership and Professional Standards Committee for investigation. Inspectors ensure that members comply with their Code of Professional Standards.

The National Association of Plumbing, Heating and Mechanical Service Contractors may also be a good point of contact. They offer a Code of Fair Trading together with a warranty scheme. The latter is a completion of work guarantee worth £500 available exclusively to NAPH & MSC members. Heating and Ventilating Contractors' Association represents central heating contractors and has a Home Heating Group Double Guarantee Scheme for members.

### Double glazing and new kitchens

Home improvements such as these are expensive undertakings. Their salesmen may be the butt of many a joke but it's no joke if you are one of their victims.

Again, use one who is a member of an association. This does not guarantee good work but you are more protected if something goes wrong. The Glass and Glazing Federation, for example, has a Five Star Customer Charter which offers advice on where and what to buy, safeguards when you buy, quality and service at all times and continuing customer care. It looks like one of the better trade association deals around. It also has a deposit indemnity fund which protects any deposit you put down.

Kitchen Specialists Association (KSA) offers ConsumerCare – an insurance-backed deposit protection scheme. All KSA members are vetted and work to an approved code of practice. The Association offers advice on what to look for when buying fitted kitchens, bedrooms and bathrooms and can provide a conciliation service.

## Decorators

Members of the British Decorators Association conform to a Code of Practice and the Association offers an arbitration service. They are subjected to spot checks.

National Federation of Painting and Decorating membership must follow a strict code of practice. If complaints arise the workman is visited by a panel who will assess the work.

## Repairs

It's not always worth having appliances repaired so check with the service organisation if there is a minimum charge. Repairs to small appliances such as toasters and kettles can cost more than a replacement. Check over large appliances before you call anyone out – the instruction manual often gives you a few ideas of what to look for. Check the expiry date of your guarantee. Give the model type and serial number to the repairer and details of the service contract.

## How to complain about a service organisation

1 If you have a complaint take it up with the service organisation first.

2 If you cannot reach an agreement try your Trading Standards Department or the Citizens' Advice Bureau. Whether they are members of a trading association or not, you are still covered by the law.

3 The Domestic Appliance Service Association (DASA) or Association of Manufacturers of Domestic Appliances (AMDEA) will investigate complaints against their members.

# MOVING HOUSE

## Estate agents

We all use estate agents at some time or another and thankfully their reputation has improved since the housing boom of the 1980s. Widening the scope of the Estate Agents Act 1979 and the Property Misdescriptions Act 1991 means we have more information, and descriptions must be more accurate. Be warned though: they are still not required to tell you anything unless asked. For example, they do not need to say if a property has been underpinned.

All estate agents must give you full details of their fees and the interest they have in the property. Whether buying or selling, visit several estate agents to get an idea of costs and quality of service.

- If selling you need to choose between sole agency, joint sole agency or multiple agency. The fee is paid to the one who sells but you'll pay more if they have to compete to sell.
- If changing from one type of agreement to another, let the estate

---

### How to complain about an estate agent

1  Write directly to the manager of the agency detailing the complaint.
2  If you do not get a satisfactory reply and the estate agent belongs to the Ombudsman for Corporate Estate Agents (OCEA) Scheme, contact 01722 333306. This covers large chains but not independent estate agents.
3 If they are not a member of the OCEA Scheme, individuals may belong to one of the following: The National Association of Estate Agents (NAEA), The Royal Institution of Chartered Surveyors (RICS) or the Incorporated Society of Valuers and Auctioneers (ISVA). Alternatively, try your local Trading Standards Department. Recently an ombudsman has been appointed to cover the larger corporate estate agents and hopefully this will extend to others in the near future.

Scotland has a slightly different system in that solicitors handle the bulk of the sales. If you have a problem, approach The Law Society of Scotland.

agent know in writing or you could end up paying two sets of fees.

## Removal companies

Ask friends and relatives or local estate agents for recommendations. Choose a removal company that is a member of the British Association of Removers (BAR). They vet their members and can deal with consumer complaints. They will come round and assess the size of the move. Point out if anything requires special handling, because you may be charged extra for this.

Obtain detailed quotations (at least three) and read their conditions carefully. For example, they may stipulate a time limit for claiming for damage or loss. Check what each quote includes, such as packing or if you have to pay overtime for long moves. Check their insurance policies because these can have several 'get out' clauses should damages occur. It may be worth using your own insurance policy – you can extend your house contents' policy. The usual limitation for notifying damages is seven days.

Many members of BAR offer a Careline Guarantee which provides up to £1,500 worth of protection against mishap to your car, goods and even your new home during the first three months of occupancy.

If you are putting your belongings into storage, check that the company is adequately protected against fire and burglary and that you are sufficiently insured.

## CAR SERVICING AND REPAIRS

The industry is represented by several trade bodies such as the Retail Motor Industry Federation or Scottish Motor Traders Association in Scotland, the Society of Motor Manufacturers and Traders and the Vehicle Builders and Repairers Association.

The garages are inspected and must meet the required standard and must agree to abide by the Motor Industry Code of Conduct. This covers the supply of new and used cars, petrol, parts and accessories and car servicing and repair. They also have a scheme for dealing with customer complaints.

---

> ### Choosing a good service organisation
>
> Expect all of the following in a service organisation:
> - written code of practice
> - quick response, within three working days
> - appointments detailing morning or afternoon slots
> - spares to enable at least 80 per cent of repairs to be completed on first visit. Check when you phone that they are familiar with the model and have a good supply of parts.
> - estimate for call-out charges, inspection and repair costs given over the phone
> - adequate safety testing of the entire appliance after repair
> - twelve months' guarantee on major appliance repairs
> - public liability insurance
> - a detailed written invoice on request
> - membership of a recognised trade association

## How to complain about car servicing or repairs

1 Refer it to the dealer concerned immediately – put your grievance in writing to the manager.

2 If you are not satisfied, write to the relevant trade association.

3 If you are still not satisfied you may ask for the matter to be referred to the Independent Arbitration Service and you will have to pay a fee depending on the size of the claim. Or contact your local Trading Standards Department.

Instead of going to arbitration you can go through the small claims procedure (*see* Chapter 1).

The Automobile Association and RAC both have approvals schemes which can help in cases of dispute. If a garage displays their logo, check that it is a current member.

If you want your car repaired after an accident, use a repairer who is a member of the Vehicle Builders and Repairers Association. Their garages are independently inspected by the AA to ensure they have adequate equipment in their workshops to cater for repairs to all brands. In cases of dispute they have a full conciliation and arbitration service funded by the association. They will try to help non-members if possible.

- Choose a garage that is a member of a motor trade association.
- Use a franchised dealer if your car is under warranty otherwise the warranty might be invalidated. Check the small print on the warranty – it may require certain work to be carried out, such as rust inspections.
- If you are not using a franchised dealer check that the car is being serviced according to the manufacturer's recommendations. Remember, though, if a problem occurs as result of the servicing, you must take this up with the garage, as your warranty will not cover it.
- Check the guarantee. Is it covered over time or mileage?
- Before work starts get a quote or estimate for the work you want done – including labour costs, parts and VAT. Tell the garage to phone you if it is going to be over their quote.
- Ask for a detailed invoice itemising work done, parts and labour costs.
- If you think you're being overcharged, or the repair is sloppy, contact the manager straight away. If they won't release the car until you pay in full write '*without prejudice*' on the bill (*see* page 56)

## UTILITIES: WATER

Because of the utilities' monopoly status, industry regulators were set up by the government to act as watchdogs. These together with various independent bodies can step in and help if you have a complaint.

**British Water** (incorporating the British Effluent and Water Association and British Water Industries Group) represents over 200 companies offering water and waste water expertise including water treatment in the home. **The Water Services Association** represents ten water companies and sewerage companies (privatised in 1989). These companies supply 75 per cent of drinking water in the UK and deal with all waste. The remaining water is supplied by 21 water supply companies (covered by the **Water Companies Association**) which have always been private concerns but supply drinking water only. The 1989 Water Act radically changed the structure of the industry and provided for regulation by three bodies:

- The National Rivers Authority – responsible for the quality of rivers, lakes and coastal waters. (The new Environment Agency will take over their responsibilities.)
- The Drinking Water Inspectorate oversees the quality of tap water.
- OFWAT (the Office of Water Services) is responsible for making sure water and sewerage companies give you a good and efficient service at a fair price. It is a government department led by the Director General of Water Services. If a company does not meet any of its legally guaranteed standards, you are entitled to compensation (normally £10). Ten regional Customer Services Committees (CSCs) represent your interests and monitor services provided by the water

---

### How to complain about water or sewerage

1 Speak or write to your local water company first. All companies have a complaints procedure – ask them for a copy.

2 If you are dissatisfied with the way it is being handled, tell them and it will be referred to a higher level.

3 OFWAT will also help free of charge. Explain the full extent of the problem to the Customer Services Committee (CSC), submitting any correspondence or evidence to date. They will look into the complaint for you and if the company is at fault they will approach the company on your behalf and give recommendations.

4 If your complaint cannot be sorted it will be referred to the Director General. 127 were considered by him in 1993–4, mostly relating to increased charges and structure changes.

5 Again, if you're dissatisfied with his handling of the situation you can go further, by approaching your Member of Parliament to take the matter to the Parliamentary Commissioner for Administration (the Parliamentary Ombudsman). Realistically, this would have to be a serious problem.

companies. They are also responsible for dealing with your complaints.

The CSCs received 40,672 inquiries in 1993–94 of which 14,792 were complaints. 44 per cent were resolved by the companies and 53 per cent by the CSCs. Most were about charges and billing.

The CSC and Director General can't deal with complaints such as:
- activities other than water and sewerage services
- quality of rivers, lakes, estuaries, etc, which fall under the domain of the National Rivers Authority
- issues which can only be decided in the courts, eg compensation claims for damages

OFWAT have a Guaranteed Standards Scheme which entitles you to payments should certain standards of service not be met.

## TELEPHONES

All the telecommunications companies are regulated by the Office of Telecommunications (OFTEL).

### British Telecom

BT publish a Customer Guarantee scheme which covers standards of service you should expect and compensation offered if they are not. For example, if an appointment is made to install a line and it is not kept you can claim compensation equivalent to one month's line rental for every day late.

---

### How to complain to BT

1  Phone 150 for sales, accounts and general complaints or 151 for repair complaints.

2  Alternatively, write to your local BT office or go into any BT shop.

3  If you do not reach a satisfactory conclusion ring BT's Complaints Review Service on 0800 545458. Or write to the Complaints Review Manager at your local BT office.

4  If you need to take the matter further refer the complaint to OFTEL.

---

If you receive malicious calls call BT's adviceline on 0800 666700. They also publish a leaflet suggesting how to handle the calls. It is available from Phone Shops, police stations, libraries or Citizens' Advice Bureaux.

## Mercury

About one million consumers now subscribe to Mercury. You still use the same BT exchange, lines and numbers but you can access Mercury through any Mercury-compatible phone using a personal access code. Mercury recommends its customers to use BT for local calls and Mercury for national and international calls, which are cheaper than BT's.

Obviously complaints with the line and exchange will be made to BT but for bill queries or telephone problems call Mercury Customer Service Centre in Manchester (0500 500194). This is open 24 hours a day. For unresolved disputes contact OFTEL.

## THE POST OFFICE

This is divided into the Royal Mail, Post Office Counters and Parcelforce. All have separate Codes of Practice, available from post offices, detailing standards of service, the complaints procedure and levels of compensation.

The consumer is represented by The Post Office Users' National

---

### How to complain about the post

1  If you have a complaint about Royal Mail, put it in writing and send it Freepost to your local Royal Mail Customer Service Centre. Alternatively, call 0345 740740.

2  For a complaint about Post Office Counters, speak to the Branch Manager or Subpostmaster, on 0345 223344, or write to the local Helpline Manager.

3  If you are not satisfied with the response write to POUNC (if in England) or the appropriate Post Office User Council for Northern Ireland, Scotland or Wales.

---

**The right package**

If you are making a claim for damage to a parcel it must have been packaged properly in the first place. Parcelforce give recommendations for the grade of outer packaging according to the weight of the contents and types of cushioning material. If this is not adequate you will lose your right to compensation. Free advice is available by calling 0800 22 44 66

---

Council (POUNC) with separate Councils for Northern Ireland, Scotland and Wales. This independent watchdog organisation has responsibility for: letter services, recorded delivery service, registered post, supply of stamps, counter services, Post Offices generally, collections, deliveries, private boxes, parcels services (limited remit).

POUNC does *not* monitor: National Girobank, time-sensitive delivery services such as Datapost, counter services where the Post Office acts as agent (such as TV and road licences), post bus services, philatelic services, Intelpost.

# GAS

British Gas's monopoly in the domestic gas supply market will start to end in 1996, when competition will be introduced into a pilot area covering Cornwall, Devon and Somerset; full competition is planned for 1998. The industry is regulated by OFGAS, whose main duty is to protect the interests of British Gas's tariff customers in matters relating to the supply of gas.

British Gas has recently divided into five business units covering its UK operations. These are: Public Gas Supply (domestic gas supply), TransCo (responsible for the gas pipeline network), Service (appliance installation, repair and servicing), Retail (appliance sales) and Business Gas (industrial and commercial gas supply). Domestic consumers' main contact will be with Public Gas Supply.

British Gas has a formal procedure for dealing with customer complaints.

Details are contained in a booklet, which is available by completing a request form from the Post Office, or from your local British Gas office.

If you have a complaint or query about your gas bill, contact your regional office, whose address and telephone number appears on your bill. British Gas aims to resolve complaints at the first contact and says it will reply to written complaints within five days. If your complaint is not resolved to your satisfaction, it can be taken up with the Area Specialist Team, which, if necessary, will consult the Customer Services Manager, who has overall responsibility for complaint handling within the region.

If you are unhappy with the response you receive from British Gas, you may take your complaint to the Gas Consumers' Council (GCC), whose details can be found on the back of your gas bill, or in the telephone directory under Gas. It has two major roles: 1) to provide information and take up complaints on behalf of consumers 2) to campaign on behalf of consumers on a wide range of gas issues. Its services are free.

If the GCC cannot help and your complaint relates to the supply of gas, you may contact OFGAS. OFGAS will investigate your case and is able to make British Gas alter its decision if it finds that the company has failed to comply with its statutory obligations.

## ELECTRICITY

Electricity is supplied by fourteen regional electricity companies in the UK which report to the Director General of Electricity Supply. The Electricity Act 1989 set out the standards we should expect and also provided a common framework across the regional companies.

The consumer is represented by Electricity Consumers' Committees (ECCs) in each region. They deal with all aspects of electricity supply, from services for the elderly to individual complaints. If the Committee is unable to resolve an issue with an electricity company it can refer the matter to the Director General of Electricity Supply.

These ECCs advise the industry regulator, the Office of Electricity

---

> ### How to complain about electricity
>
> 1 To complain, contact your local electricity supply company by phone or in writing using the contacts list on the back of your bill.
>
> 2 If you are still not happy contact your local Consumers' Committee or OFFER. There are fourteen regional offices, whose addresses can be found on the back of the electricity bill.
>
> To give you an idea of the compensation to expect, failure to restore supply within 24 hours is £40 and a missed appointment £20.

Regulation (OFFER). They will also take up issues with the companies and OFFER on behalf of the customer.

# THE NATIONAL HEALTH SERVICE

As in all big organisations the structure of the National Health Service must be understood if you are to find the right person to deal with. The National Health Service is managed locally by **NHS Authorities** which in turn have sections covering different areas:

- **Family Health Services Authorities** are responsible for the services provided by family doctors (GPs), dentists, opticians and pharmacists.
- **District Health Authorities** are responsible for the hospital and community health services provided for your district. The **Community Health Councils** represent NHS users and will advise you of your rights. They can explain how the different NHS complaints procedures work, give advice on the best way forward, help you draw up a written complaint, make sure the right people take it up, and go with you to meetings or formal hearings. Look under Community in the phone book or ring their helpline: 0800 665544.
- **Regional Health Authorities** are concerned with planning, ambulance provision and some other services direct to the public.

- **Special Health Authorities** manage certain specialist hospitals or have particular functions such as The Special Hospitals Service Authority, The Disablement Services Authority, The Health Education Authority and the London postgraduate teaching hospitals.
- **NHS Trusts** manage certain NHS hospitals or other units.

---

### Types of complaints

They will investigate:

- inadequate service from the authority or Trust
- failure to provide a service
- maladministration including not following procedures, rules or agreed policies, giving incorrect or inadequate information and long delays in replying to complaints
- attitudes and actions of a member of staff
  You will need to prove (ie you will need hard evidence) that the inadequate service or maladministration has caused you hardship or injustice.

The Ombudsman cannot investigate:

- complaints made by public service bodies, nationalised industries or any other body with members appointed by the State or which is mainly funded with the money provided by Parliament
- a complaint which could go – or could have gone – to a court or appeal to an independent tribunal, unless the Ombudsman thinks it unreasonable to expect you to do so
- clinical decisions about the care or treatment of a patient (which falls under the clinical complaints procedure, where the patient's care or treatment is reviewed by two independent consultants)
- services provided by GPs, dentists, opticians, pharmacists
- action taken by a family health service
- complaints about staff appointments, pay, pensions and discipline
- complaint about the NHS authority's commerical or contractual dealings
- out-of-date complaints (over a year)
- complaints not put right by the Authority or Trust concerned

## How to complain about the NHS

According to the Patients' Charter, everyone has the right to complain about the NHS and have their case looked at promptly and replied to in writing. However, the complaints procedure can be quite long-winded and slow. This does not cover problems with services covered by your local GP – that procedure is slightly different (*see* page 75).

All hospitals now have a specialist **Complaints Officer** whose job it is to deal with queries. But having said that, each hospital's system may be slightly different. If you are unsure what to do, contact your local Community Health Council. If you have a complaint about an NHS authority or Trust, which has not been satisfactorily resolved by that body you may put your complaint to the **Health Service Commissioner** or **Ombudsman**. He is independent of the NHS, an officer of Parliament, and reports regularly to a select committee at the House of Commons.

## Complaints procedure

1 First talk to the staff involved – you may be able to settle the problem there and then. If you can't, then put your complaint in writing (keeping a copy for yourself) and send it to the complaints officer or to the general manager of the NHS Authority or Trust concerned. Do this immediately you have a problem. Clearly state the following:
- your name, date of birth or hospital number
- date and details of the incident
- names of the staff involved or a description of them
- the nature of your complaint and the issues you want investigated

Give the NHS authority a reasonable time to reply and look into your complaint – at least a month to be realistic.

2 If you get no joy from the NHS Authority then write to the Ombudsman. Again include all the details as listed above plus copies of correspondence you have had with the Authority. You must make your complaints within one year of their first arising.

3 The Ombudsman provides a free service and will:
- decide whether or not he can investigate your complaint (if not you will be sent a letter explaining why not)

- take up your case. His officers will draw up a summary of the complaint and a copy will be sent to you and the NHS authority concerned
- meet with you to discuss the case and keep you informed of progress
- possibly re-imburse you for travel expenses if you need to attend interviews. Procedures are informal.
- send you a written report at the end of the investigation. If he finds your complaint to be justified, the report will give details of what the NHS Authority has agreed to do to remedy any injustice or hardship caused.

**4** If the problem is about *standards of hospital care*, send your complaint in writing to the Complaints Officer as soon as possible. (There is no time restriction but obviously the fresher it is in your memory the better.)

The Complaints Officer will follow up your query. Expect at least a written explanation and apology if the complaint is justified. Hopefully most problems can be sorted out at this stage.

**5** If you wish to take the matter further it can be forwarded to the **Regional Medical Officer** who will decide whether to investigate by holding an **Independent Professional Review**. Here two doctors from other districts will consider your case. You can have friends or your GP with you for moral support and to advise.

If they decide that the incident was handled correctly they will explain why it was treated in that way. If not they will discuss it with the Regional Health Officer and let you know the outcome. This could include an apology and outline steps being taken to prevent it from recurring. There could be disciplinary action. If you are not happy you can go to the Ombudsman.

**6** For complaints about non-medical hospital services (eg catering, hygiene, facilities, maintenance, information, waiting times, visiting and discharge arrangements and staff provision), complain to the general hospital or chief executive (if you were treated at a trust). Send a copy to the general manager of the health authority.

**7** For complaints about clinical care (eg care provided by health professionals working at a hospital or as part of a community service run by a health authority or trust – community services include clinics, community nurses or health visitors), complain to the general manager of the unit. Send a copy to the general manager of the health authority. If the complaint is serious it may be referred to the regional director of public health for an independent professional review.

## Doctors (GPs)

Like many other professions, GPs are now encouraged to have their own code of practice covering things like waiting times and standards of service. The Patients' Charter covers GPs as well as hospital care.

The Family Health Services Authority (FHSA) has encouraged surgeries to have more information available for their patients. You should be able to obtain information leaflets explaining the practice policies, appointment procedures and what to do in case of an emergency.

**Appointments** How many times have you made an appointment to see your GP for a set time, arrived promptly but still had to wait over half an hour? This is common whether they have an appointment system or more of a first-come first-served policy.

**If you have a complaint about a GP** Talk to your doctor first – or, if you'd prefer, follow the formal or informal complaints procedure set up by the FHSA. Their address must be displayed in your local surgery, and it will also be in the phone book. You must do this within 13 weeks of the incident. Alternatively someone can do this for you if you are too ill.

Wherever possible, the FHSA will try to settle the complaint informally with the help of a conciliator. They may need to carry out a formal investigation if the doctor has acted negligently or not followed his terms of service. Formal investigations are carried out by the Service Committee, which consists of medical and non-medical representatives and is chaired by a layperson. They may need to hold a hearing to get both sides of the story. It will be quite informal, but you can get someone else to stand in for you if you are ill or feel you can't cope with it.

The results of the hearing or investigation will be forwarded to the FHSA, who will then decide if your complaint is justified. If the doctor is at fault he will either be given a formal warning, have pay deducted or be referred to a professional body for disciplinary action.

If you are unhappy with any aspect of your local surgery but don't have any specific incidents to complain about, you may find it more satisfactory simply to change doctors. You are fully entitled to do this but a doctor can refuse to have you on his list. Before you register, check their information leaflets to see if this practice is more in line with your needs.

**Complaints about professional conduct** These can include neglect, charging for free services, excessive drinking, a sexual or emotional relationship with a patient, or mental or physical illness.

These complaints are made to the General Medical Council (GMC), which is made up of medical and non-medical members. All qualified doctors from a recognised medical school in the UK or EC can register. It has strong disciplinary powers but only covers those doctors who are members and are involved in serious misconduct cases. A doctor can be struck off its list if found guilty of certain misdemeanours.

The GMC does not deal with midwives, dentists or nurses; administration staff; administration of NHS services or private hospitals.

---

### Complaining to the GMC

The GMC will:
- consider a complaint from anyone, without time limits (remember though the longer you leave it the harder it is to prove)
- act on complaints of serious professional misconduct by named doctors
- provide legal representation for you at public hearings

The GMC will *not*:
- review reports of doctors, clinical misjudgement – this must be dealt with in the civil courts with legal representation
- investigate doctors' charges or fees for services
- award compensation if the doctor is found guilty
- investigate complaints about a doctor's social behaviour

1 If you feel your doctor has acted improperly write to the GMC giving the following information (and keeping a copy for yourself):
- full name and address of the doctor concerned
- precise details of what the doctor is alleged to have done, or failed to do
- dates of events
- copies of any correspondence supporting your claim, or other supporting evidence such as tape recordings or photographs
- names and address of any witnesses

2 A member of the Council will decide if the claim is valid and can be proved.

3 If it is, you will be asked to make a sworn statement, in the form of an affidavit or statutory declaration, to support your complaint. You will have to pay a fee for making this sworn statement.

4 These statements are sent for comments, to the doctor named in the complaint. The complaint and comments then go to the GMC's **Preliminary Proceedings Committee**. This committee is made up of members of the GMC and a senior barrister to advise on points of law. They meet in private three times a year and are confidential to the GMC, complainant and doctor. They decide whether the case should be referred to the **Professional Conduct Committee (PCC)**. You won't need to attend and you'll be notified as soon as possible of the outcome. If the case is not referred, a letter of warning may be sent to the doctor about his conduct or no further action be taken.

5 If you are referred to the PCC, the GMC will offer you legal representation or you may want to represent yourself. Legal Aid is not available for the Council's disciplinary proceedings.

6 The doctor is then formally charged on the basis of your complaint. Evidence is given on oath and you may be cross-examined by the defending lawyer and questioned by the members of the PCC. The PCC consists of members of the GMC and a senior barrister to advise on points of law. They meet in the Council's offices in London, usually in March, July and November, each year. Meetings are public and cases may be reported in the media. Proceedings are similar to a criminal court, and the doctor and complainant (with legal representation) both attend.

**7** As in a criminal court, the charge has to be proved beyond reasonable doubt and the PCC must decide if it amounted to serious professional misconduct. If the complaint is upheld the doctor can be subjected to certain conditions such as retraining in some aspects, suspended for a set period or struck off the register.

**8** The doctor has 28 days to appeal to the Judicial Committee of the Privy Council. If it appears that the doctor is unfit to practise due to ill health he is referred to the Health Committee.

The PCC can't award compensation – if you still have the energy this must be pursued through the civil courts subject to legal advice.

## Dentists

When choosing a dentist you need to decide whether you want to be treated as a private patient or through the NHS. Check first if you're exempt from payment (you'll find explanatory leaflets in post offices). Most dentists do private treatment only (apart from children's teeth), so check first. If the dentist has agreed to treat you on the NHS you must sign an application form agreeing to be treated for at least two years (called 'continuing care'). He or she is then obliged to treat you under the NHS – the contract can be extended every two years as necessary. However, you'll still have to pay, and costs are not hugely different.

After each check-up your dentist should give you a treatment plan and charge estimate. You will be charged for the check-up, any X-rays, advice and hygienist treatment. If you want a second opinion ask for it – your dentist will refer you to another NHS dentist or to a dental hospital. You may of course wish to go for a private examination.

If anything goes wrong within 12 months of NHS work being carried out on your teeth, for example, if your filling comes loose after six months, you can have it put right free of charge – if you are still with the same dentist or practice. This does not include accidents or temporary work.

**How to complain about a dentist** Try to sort things out directly with your dentist. If this doesn't help, contact your local Family Health Services Authority within 13 weeks of the incident. If you are still unable to resolve your complaint and there is evidence of serious professional misconduct, you should write to the **General Dental Council**, which looks at each case individually. If they feel your case is justified they will send you details of their complaints procedure. However, they don't deal with compensation so you would have to go to court for that.

## Opticians

Optometrists or ophthalmic opticians are qualified to test sight and prescribe glasses, and fit and supply glasses and contact lenses, whereas a dispensing optician can only fit and supply glasses and, if qualified, contact lenses.

You must pay a charge for the sight test unless exempt under the NHS scheme. You can use that prescription in any shop. You may prefer to use an express service or perhaps you like a frame you've seen elsewhere. Shop around because prices vary tremendously.

**How to complain about an optician** First talk to the optician to try and resolve the problem calmly. If you have a complaint about a prescription carried out under the NHS, go to your local Family Health Services Authority.

If your complaint is about the standard of product or test, go to the **Optical Consumer Complaint Service** (0171-261 1017).

If your complaint is more serious (ie misconduct) you are required to write to the **General Optical Council**. Out of the 11 million tests carried out in the UK they only receive about one hundred complaints.

## CHILD CARE PROBLEMS

If you are accused, or involved in, any of the following cases seek legal advice immediately. Contact the Law Society who have a list of lawyers specialising in these types of cases.

- Problems in sorting out responsibility and contact with children following divorce or separation. Where agreement is difficult the court can make orders dealing with residence and contact. It can also prohibit certain steps such as changing a child's name, and can help deal with issues such as religion, schooling and medical treatment.

- Abduction
- Care proceedings. A local authority may seek to take a child into care where they rightly or wrongly feel the child is suffering significant harm (or is likely to suffer harm) and the harm is the result of a lack of parental care or of the child being beyond parental control.
- If you have been accused of abusing your child.
- Children born outside marriage. Parental responsibilities rest entirely with the mother unless a specific agreement or court order has been made giving parental control to the father. A mother may be able to apply for maintenance payments from the father.

### Child-minders
All child-minders must be registered with the local authority. If problems with a child-minder can't be sorted out with them directly, contact the social services department of your local authority. For further information or advice contact the **National Childminding Association**.

## EDUCATION

### The Parents' Charter
The Parents' Charter lays out the standards you should expect from schools and methods of sorting out problems. You are entitled to:

- a report about your child at least once a year
- a report about the school from independent inspectors who monitor standards in schools
- performance tables for all your local schools (including LEA-maintained schools, grant-maintained schools, City Technology Colleges and some independent schools)
- a prospectus or brochure about individual schools
- an annual report from the school's governors.
  The Parents' Charter includes details of:
- subject selection and the National Curriculum. The National

Curriculum was brought in to raise standards of educational provision and increase accountability to parents. It brings with it a route for complaining. Schools must have a published complaints procedure and all Local Education Authorities must have a Complaints Officer.

- testing and examinations
- what you should expect from a secondary school in terms of advice on choices at age 14 and 16 and career guidance.

The Parents' Charter gives you the right:

- to vote for parent governors and to stand for election yourself
- to go to the annual parents' meeting
- to vote on whether the school should apply for grant-maintained status.

---

### Schools explained

- **Local Education Authority (LEA) maintained schools** The governors and headteachers are responsible for the running of the school but the budget is set by the local council. The council will also mediate if things go wrong.
- **Voluntary-aided schools** Many of these are church schools and usually encourage some form of religious belief. Funded by the local council and outside agencies such as the Church, or brewers' or drapers' guilds.
- **Grant-maintained schools** Run by headteachers and governors. These are free state schools which are independent of the local authority. They get their money direct from central government.
- **City Technology Colleges (CTCs)** Set up in towns and cities funded from Government and with investment from businesses, these concentrate on technology and science.
- **Selective school**s Entrance is restricted to the more academically able children.
- **Independent schools** These are fee-paying schools, though some have a few assisted places where central government pays all or part of the pupil's fees depending on the parents' income. This will obviously be selective – only those who excel in entrance exams will be considered.

## What to look for when choosing a school
- Look at school prospectuses, exam results, attendance records, governors' reports and inspectors' reports.
- Visit the school during term time, as well as open evenings. Look at classroom displays, equipment, maintenance of buildings and ground, amount of litter, general appearance and demeanour of pupils and teachers.
- atmosphere (and noise levels) of playground, corridors, classrooms
- teacher/pupil relationships

Find out about the school's
- range of subjects taught/extra-curricular activities
- provision for the most and least able pupils
- discipline/rules/school policy on homework, uniform, assessment
- class sizes
- amount of parental involvement

## Applying for a place in a state secondary school
Finding the right school is every parents' nightmare. According to the Updated Parents' Charter (DFE, 1994) 'you have a right to a place in the school you want unless all the places at the school have been given to pupils who have a stronger claim to a place at that school.'

It is possible for parents to apply for places in the schools of several different authorities. In a 1989 test case, it was established that a Local Education Authority cannot discriminate against children resident in other boroughs. However, some popular schools apply certain entry criteria which ensure particular parents are successful.

In six of the former ILEA (Inner London Education Authority) boroughs a banding system (based on a test of verbal reasoning), designed to theoretically give an academically balanced intake to each school, still operates. Once a band is full, no more children of that academic level are considered unless places are unfilled.

In other schools there are various ways in which priority is given for places; you should find these listed in the school prospectus. The prospectus should always publish how many parents applied for places for their children and how many got in every year. In some areas, proximity to school is a strong factor in favour of the applicant. This may mean moving house, but even that will not guarantee a place.

In areas where places in the best state schools are quickly filled, your only option if you can afford it may be to choose a fee-paying school.

If your child has special educational needs because of disability or learning difficulty, the Parents' Charter states that he or she has a 'right to an education which meets those needs', in an ordinary school where possible. You may, however, feel your child would be better provided for in a special school – if in an assessment this is deemed to be the case, the local council will pay for the place if the school is fee-paying.

## Complaints procedure for state schools

**1** Make an informal complaint to the school itself whether it is to the teacher concerned, to the form teacher or to the headteacher. If the complaint is about the LEA talk to the appropriate officers of the authority. Generally the head teacher should be approached before a formal complaint is registered. Obviously this does not apply if the complaint is about the headteacher or governing body.

**2** Make a formal complaint to the governing body. A complaints panel (consisting of three to five governors) will meet when necessary to consider the problem. The verdict of the panel will be given in writing with information on how to take the complaint further if necessary.

**3** Where the complaint is about a governing body, or where you are not happy with the outcome from the first two stages, you can approach the Complaints Officer of the LEA.

## What to do if ...

**... your child doesn't get a place** If your child isn't offered a place at the state school of your preference, you can appeal – details are available from the governing body or LEA. If you think the appeal was not conducted correctly, you can make a complaint to the Local Government Ombudsman in England. If your appeal has been unsuccessful you still have the right to complain to the Secretary of State. He can make the school offer you a place if he feels it is justified. Contact the Parents' Charter Unit in the Department for Education.

**... you have problems with the curriculum** You may, for example, not wish for your child to study religious education or take part in collective worship in school. Appeal to the governors first and then to the local council. For a grant-maintained school, direct complaints straight to the governors. You have the right to ensure that your child is excluded from certain lessons such as sex education or religious studies, so long as they are not part of the National Curriculum.

**... your child is expelled or suspended** Discipline is the responsibility of the headteacher. If a head feels a child should be suspended or expelled they have the power to do so. They must detail the incident to you fully, and most schools will ask to meet the parent or guardian to discuss behaviour problems. You can appeal to the governing body or in the case of expulsion to a special committee, if the governing body or local council agree with the expulsion. If you think the appeal was conducted improperly try your Local Government Ombudsman. If you are going to proceed further do be sure of your facts.

**... you are querying your child's public exam results** Get the school to contact the examining body. If, after following their appeals procedure, you are still unhappy, try the Independent Appeals Authority for School Examinations. The school can appeal on your behalf. However, they cannot re-mark the examination – they will just step in if the examining body's procedures have been at fault.

You can re-enter your child for an examination but you'll have to pay the examination fee if the school does not agree with you.

## Changing school

If you are unhappy with the school you are fully entitled to transfer your child to another school but often this is easier said than done. For instance, the new school must have a spare place – the best schools are often over-subscribed. Also, you must think what is best for your child. Transferring them to another school at secondary level can be very disruptive.

If your concerns are about the school's general standards, try discussing your worries with other parents to obtain support. Then approach one of the governors to have the complaint considered. The governing body has the overall responsibility for the conduct of the school.

## Independent schools

There are currently about 2,400 registered independent schools. These educate about 7.4 per cent of the school-going population. All must be registered with the Department for Education and satisfy their basic recommendations. Apart from this they are totally independent of central and local government intervention except in cases of law.

In 1980, the Independent Schools Joint Council, representing the main associations associated with independent schools, set up a system for accrediting schools in membership of these associations. To become accredited they must pass an inspection carried out by a team headed by former HMSIs (School inspectors). The associations include: The Headmasters Conference (HMC); Society of Headmasters and Headmistresses of Independent Schools (SHMIS); Governing Bodies Association (GBA); Girls' Schools Association (GSA); Governing Bodies of Girls' Schools Association (GBGSA); Incorporated Association of Preparatory Schools (IAPS); Independent Schools Association Incorporated (ISAI).

Although independent schools are fee-paying, it may be possible to obtain:

• **Scholarships** Many schools will offer several places for children who excel in their entrance exams.

• **Assisted places** (about 5,700 available every year). Introduced by the government in 1981, this scheme was set up to help parents with the cost of tuition at certain independent schools. Most assisted places are awarded at the ages of 11 and 13 although there are also some places for pupils going straight into the sixth form. Schools actually select the pupils themselves so you must apply directly to the school. Children are subject to an entrance exam and interview. The actual amount of financial assistance given depends on the family income. For more detailed information contact the relevant schools and the Department for Education (Assisted Places Team).

• **Bursaries** Sometimes grants known as bursaries are given by schools to help you pay the fees. They are awarded according to a means test. For information on accredited schools, school fees, educational endowments, covenants and investment advice contact the Independent Schools Information Service (ISIS).

**Choosing an independent school** is similar to that for selecting a state school, but you will also have to consider location, fees, day v boarding, co-education v single-sex (some boys' schools now accept girls in the sixth form), choice of subjects taught (remember, an independent school does not have to follow the National Curriculum) and so on. Read prospectuses and school reports carefully.

One of the major differences between the independent and state systems is the power of the parent. The head of an independent school is responsible to the governors but knows at the end of the day if you don't like any aspect of the school's policy or teaching methods you will send your child elsewhere. Complaints procedures are therefore less complicated than in the state system. Problems will be sorted out by the teachers and governors within the school. Because of this the schools are self-monitored and self-regulating.

# GENERAL SERVICES

### Dry-cleaners
• When you take an item to the dry-cleaners you must remember to point out any specific stains or unusual fabrics.
• Avoid treating a stain yourself first, because this may fix it. If you have tried to remove it, tell the cleaner what you used.
• Remove any unusual or ornate trimmings.
• Point out any dry-cleaning symbol which is underlined because this tells the dry-cleaner that a special treatment is required.
• You may find that some stains, such as colourless spills that contain

sugar-lemonade or alcohol, only show up after dry-cleaning because they have been brought out by the solvents used. These may not be removable.

## What to do if things go wrong:

1 Make a formal complaint, in writing, to the manager of the company, explaining the problem; keep copies of your correspondence.
2 If you don't hear anything after ten days, or are not satisfied with the response, ask for help from your Citizens' Advice Bureau or Trading Standards Department.
3 If you don't seem to be getting anywhere, contact the Textile Services Association (TSA). If the cleaner is a member, the Association's Customer Advisor will help with the problem. However, if the problem is difficult to resolve and you are determined to sort it out, it is advisable to have the garment analysed by an independent test laboratory (see Addresses). You will be charged for this service, but should the cleaner be found to have been negligent you will be reimbursed and compensated. The Fabric Care Research Association will charge you around £78 for analysis and their report can be used in a court of law. To give you an idea of what to claim for, a woman's or gent's suit up to three months old which has only been cleaned once is classed as new.
4 If the dry-cleaners is not an Association member the Citizens' Advice Bureau will suggest your next step. Most probably this will be the small claims procedure (*see* page 8) if they feel you have a strong enough case. Again, you will need to have an analysis carried out.

Under the terms laid out by the Office of Fair Trading, dry-cleaners have a legal duty 'to provide their service with reasonable care and skill and in a reasonable time'. If this is not followed you are entitled to part or all of your money back.

## Launderettes

The case is very slightly different if your dispute is about a service wash carried out in a launderette. The contract, as in the case of a dry-cleaner, is not for a single item but for the bag of laundry. It is your responsibility therefore to put everything that is to be washed at the same temperature in the same bag. If a garment runs it is not the washer's fault as the contract relates to the whole bag.

Loss of items is more difficult to resolve. To prevent problems occurring, draw up a list and get the washer to sign and agree to the contents.

## Hairdressers

According to the National Hairdressers' Federation around 50 million people visit a hairdresser in any three-month period. Inevitably there is going to be some cause for complaint. Unfortunately, the industry is not regulated, so anyone can set themselves up as a hairdresser whatever their background and experience.

Some hairdressers are State Registered through the Hairdressers' Council, which means they must have successfully completed a nationally recognised two-year course or three-year apprenticeship. Look out for their logo in the salon – remember that it is awarded to individuals not the whole salon so check it is *your* hairdresser who is registered. Interestingly, only in three EC countries can hairdressers practise without any training or qualifications – the UK, Ireland and Greece.

**When things go wrong** 1994 saw a glut of sensationalist headlines such as 'Hairdressers from hell', sparked off by a series of successful compensation claims.

If you aren't happy with the result of a cut or treatment – for example, you feel it isn't a good cut or highlights aren't very visible – then let the person who did your hair know immediately. A good salon should offer to rectify the problem at this stage. If complaining to your stylist doesn't work then go directly to the manager.

If you accept a refund from a hairdresser this does not stop you from claiming at a later date if your hair starts to deteriorate as a result of a treatment. But if you are worried you could ask them to sign an agreement stating this. Alternatively do not sign anything they ask you to, in case it stops you claiming further. Don't try any remedial action yourself – it may make matters worse.

If you are dissatisfied deduct a reasonable amount from the bill. If you feel you want to take the claim further because it is more serious – burns, hair loss, etc – you will probably have to get legal advice. First of all write to them threatening court action – but remember, court action will cost you money, so be prepared to carry out the threat. If your hairdresser is State Registered, contact the Hairdressers' Council, who may be able to help you by liaising with the hairdresser on your behalf. They can threaten to deregister them – not a great deterrent as they can still work.

Make sure you collect plenty of evidence – take photos of the areas, take samples of your hair, consult your GP if the skin or scalp is burnt. It may even be worth consulting a trichologist for advice. (You will have to pay for this but should be able to claim this back off the hairdresser if your case is upheld.)

If you're claiming up to £1,000 compensation go through the small claims procedure. Use the county courts if it's more than £1,000.

By the same token, if you don't keep an appointment they are entitled to claim compensation or charge a penalty fee.

**Remember:** Be persistent. Don't be put off by the hairdressers' reluctance to accept responsibility – they are responsible.

## Hotels

Descriptions of hotels, like other goods, must comply with the Trade Descriptions Acts 1968 and 1972. Should discrepancies arise, notify your local Trading Standards Department.

Places which provide accommodation are required by law to display prices, have suitable fire precautions and have facilities for safeguarding valuables.

Even if the hotel has star ratings by various organisations such as the English Tourist Board, AA and RAC, most include disclaimers should they not live up to expectation.

Basically it's up to you to complain to the management as soon as you are dissatisfied. Don't wait until you return home because this will weaken your case. Some Tourist Boards may help with certain complaints – it's worth asking for their opinion if the hotel has been approved by them. However, they have no statutory power to do anything.

Telephone charges are a frequent cause for complaint. Hotel unit

---

### Valuables

Always put valuables in the hotel safe so that if anything happens the hotel is responsible, not you. Many hotels will disclaim responsibility for items brought on to their premises by guests and have a notice to this effect in their hotel. However, under the Hotel Proprietors Act the owner is liable for the value of the loss or damage to any guest's property but if the proprietor has a notice his liability is limited to the sum of £50 for one article and not more than £100 per guest. Of course, this doesn't apply if the article was in the hotel's safekeeping or if the negligence or damage was deliberate on the part of the hotel's employees.

---

charges are often higher than standard telephone company charges – they say it's to cover their costs. There is no restriction on what they can charge so check with reception how these differ from standard charges. Those hotels recommended by the English Tourist Board are required to display the charges by the phones or in the room information pack.

## Restaurants

Many of us avoid complaining in restaurants because the threat of an argument can spoil the ambience, especially if we are out celebrating with family and friends. But we should – it's in our and the restaurant's best interest to do so. The restaurant may not realise they are not living up to expectations or they may think they can get away with less than the best. You must complain at the time and when you complain be positive.

You should expect:

- A reasonable standard of presentation and service.
- A waiter should attend your table within five minutes of being seated.
- If you have booked a table you should not have to wait more than 15 minutes without at least being offered a drink.
- After ordering, the waiting time depends very much on what you have ordered and the type of restaurant. If you are looking forward to home-prepared fresh food, don't expect express service.

You should complain about:

---

### Remember

If making a booking at a hotel or restaurant in writing or by phone, you are entering into a legally binding contract. They can demand payment if you fail to take up the booking. In the case of hotels it's worth considering cancellation insurance (this may be a condition of the booking).

---

- chipped plates, dirty cutlery, smeary glasses, being seated near toilets or the kitchen, overloud music.
- wine served at the wrong temperature. Don't forget some red wine should be chilled and white wine shouldn't be over-cold.
- poor food and service. You can refuse to pay; however, if they insist you'll have to leave your name and address. If they call the police they cannot prosecute because it is a civil dispute. If they lock you in the restaurant or threaten you, you are justified in calling the police.
- hygiene. These complaints should be relayed to your local department of the environment.
- suspected cases of food poisoning can be difficult to prove because some strains do not appear until 72 hours after eating. You have to prove without doubt that it was that particular meal that caused the problem. Obviously a whole party going down with sickness is a reasonably conclusive case! Again, this should be dealt with by the local environmental health officer.
- cold coffee. It's surprising the number of people who will accept lukewarm coffee after a meal.
- mischarging on bills is common so always check. Itemised bills give less cause for argument.

## Photography

Many of us don't complain when we've had photos developed which are disappointing – frequently blaming our own amateur use of the camera. However, it may be faulty equipment or film, poor repair or processing.

**Remember:** Always use developers and retailers who are members of the photographic trade associations. This means they are covered by a code of practice called the Photocode.

**Films** As incentives to buy films or have photos developed many companies offer free films or buy-two-and-get-one-free. Always read the small print of the offer.

**Processing** This can be done by the shop or through mail order outlets. Prices should be clearly displayed. Be sure of what you are getting – size of print, colour, finish, etc. Always get a receipt. If it's a valuable film it might be advisable to go to a specialist laboratory. Indeed some places may not accept the responsibility for them or charge you extra.

If you are not happy with the quality compare your print with the negative using a magnifying glass.

The type of problems that can occur include: processors cutting down the picture too much; marks and blotches on the negative. These could be the result of chemical splashes during developing. Tears and scratches may be from machinery damage. Try again with a second film; if similar things happen, your camera is at fault. If the negative is perfect but the print has white spots or hairs the processor is at fault. If you are dissatisfied with the colour ask the processor to repeat the process – most will do this free of charge. If the lighting looks wrong, have a reprint done but bear in mind that you may simply have under- or over-exposed it.

**Lost film** Always stick your name and address on the film itself or, to be very sure, photograph your name and address on the first exposure. If your film is lost, compensation is usually limited to the cost of the film only.

**Photographers** When choosing a photographer, if you can't get recommendations from friends look for members of the British Institute of Professional Photography or Master Photographers' Association. Always ask to see examples of their work and get a full breakdown of their fees and delivery dates before you agree to take them on.

If you are dissatisfied with any service, do the following:

1 Contact the shop, processor, repairer or photographer immediately. Take a receipt or proof of purchase with you and any evidence to support your complaint. In most cases the problem will be rectified at once.

2 If not, talk the problem over at your local Citizens' Advice Bureau or Trading Standards Department.

3 If the company is a Photocode member you can ask their trade body to try and help settle the dispute. Photocode provides for low-cost, independent arbitration. You'll pay a registration fee but you get it back if your claim succeeds. Or you can take action in the small claims court. You can't go to an arbitrator and court.

If you are unable to get immediate satisfaction from the company, approach one of the following for help:

• Film or equipment queries – The British Photographic Association

• Processing queries – The National Pharmaceutical Association

• Repair queries – The Institute of Photographic Apparatus Repair Technicians; Photo Marketing Associates International UK.

### Funeral services

If you can, choose a funeral director who is registered with either:

• the **National Association of Funeral Directors** which has a code of practice drawn up in consultation with the Office of Fair Trading. They operate a conciliation and arbitration procedure.

• the **Funeral Standards Council** which has set up an ombudsman to deal with consumer complaints and raise standards within the industry.

Funeral costs involve paying for the funeral directors' services (collecting and caring for the body) and the disbursements that you choose (cremation fee, church service fee, etc). They should give you a written estimate before the funeral and give you an itemised bill at the end. A basic funeral should be available which includes the coffin, conveyance from a local address, care of the deceased, provision of a hearse and one following car and the attention of the funeral director to all the arrangements. Costs vary depending on the region and the company.

If you have a complaint, tell the funeral director. Should he be unable to resolve the matter, contact his trade association if he is a member. They will conciliate for you or carry out further investigations. If necessary you can pay the relevant fee to use an arbitration scheme. If they are not members, go to your local Trading Standards Department who can advise.

If you go to the Ombudsman (ie if your funeral company is a member of the Funeral Standards Association) he can award compensation up to £50,000 and ensure that the company changes its procedures if applicable.

# EMERGENCY SERVICES

### Police

Police officers are subject not only to criminal and civil law but also to their own statutory disciplinary code, which covers all aspects of their contact with the public (discreditable conduct, abuse of authority, discrimination, improper disclosure of information, neglect of duty etc.).

According to the Police and Criminal Evidence Act 1984 (PACE), a Chief Officer must record and investigate all complaints made from a member of the public concerning the conduct of a member of their force. This, however, does not cover policy decisions, ie complaints regarding the control or direction of a force by its Chief Officer.

A complaint may be made personally by a complainant or by a third party (a solicitor or representative from the Citizens' Advice Bureau, for example), authority for which should be given in writing.

Complaints fall into two main categories:

• an allegation of criminal conduct by a police officer eg assault, theft, corruption, etc
• an allegation which may involve breach of the discipline code, eg incivility or rudeness, or failing to properly investigate a crime.

**Serious complaints** The complaint will be investigated by a police officer from the force's Complaints and Discipline Unit. In serious cases the investigation will be supervised by a member of the Police Complaints Authority (PCA), a statutory body whose members are independent of the police. Their purpose is to supervise (not conduct) the investigation which may be carried out by an officer from another force.

**Less serious complaints** A full investigation is held as above, but not supervised by the PCA, which may result in a disciplinary hearing.

After the conclusion of the supervised or unsupervised complaint investigation, the report, if it contains evidence of a criminal act, will be sent to the Crown Prosecution Service who will decide whether the officer will face criminal charges. The PCA have the power to request additional information and to recommend or direct the Chief Officer to prefer disciplinary charges against the officer. The charge must be proved 'beyond reasonable doubt' and if proved can result in dismissal, reduction in rank, a fine or an official reprimand.

Any minor complaints may be dealt with by a procedure called an informal resolution. This is where the complaint is reasonably trivial, such as 'I didn't like the way that policeman spoke to me'. This will normally involve discussing your complaint with an Inspector at the local police station or you can be visited at home. The Inspector, acting as a conciliator, will speak to the officer concerned and seek their point of view. If the complainant does not agree to informal resolution, the Inspector will record the details of the complaint, and submit it to the force's Complaints and Discipline Unit through his Superintendent; a full investigation will then follow.

**How to make a complaint about the police** Do one of the following:
1 Go to your local police station in person and ask to speak to the Duty Inspector regarding a complaint against police.
2 Telephone the local police station and ask for the Inspector as above.
3 Telephone your local force's headquarters and ask for the Complaints and Discipline Unit.
4 Write to the Superintendent at the local station.
5 Go to a Law Centre, solicitor, or CAB.
Always have as much of the following information available as possible.
• The date, time and place of the incident or occurrence that is the subject of the complaint.
• The name, number or description of any officer you wish to complain

about, and details such as: Were they on foot patrol? Or what type of vehicle?

- Details of anyone who may have witnessed the event.
- You should retain any note you made about what happened.

Redress may also be obtained by bringing a civil action for damages against the police. Remember though that a police officer also has rights and if the complaint is shown to be malicious or vindictive they also have a right to seek damages for this.

## Ambulances

The ambulance service is covered by the Citizens' Charter. This details all the targets they expect to meet. Ambulances are the responsibility of your local Regional Health Authority so contact them if you have cause for complaint. Initially go to the Chief Ambulance Officer for the area from which the ambulance was sent. There are no fixed compensation levels or penalties should these targets not be met.

## Fire brigade

There are 65 fire brigades in the UK. They are the responsibility of the local authority (specifically, the Local Fire Authority). According to the Citizens' Charter, there are set response targets which they must adhere to. These vary with the region. For example, the response times in London will be shorter than in the middle of the Pennines. Each fire brigade is required to do 'practice runs' to ensure they can reach their targets.

If you do have a complaint with a fire station, first contact, in writing, the Chief Fire Officer or the Chief Executive of your Local Fire Authority.

If they can't help or you are unhappy with the outcome, ask your local councillor (numbers available from council offices, libraries or Citizens' Advice Bureaux). You can also complain to the Local Government Ombudsman, who will investigate complaints free of charge. He or she will investigate whether there has been maladministration, neglect, unjustified delay and failure to follow the Council's agreed policies, rules and procedure.

# USEFUL ADDRESSES

## Education

**Boarding Schools Association**
27 Marylebone Road
London NW1 5JW
Telephone: 0171 487 3660

**Department For Education**
Assisted Places Team
Mowden Hall
Darlington
County Durham DL3 9BG
Telephone: 01325 392163

**ISIS**
56 Buckingham Gate
London SW1E 6AG
Telephone: 0171 630 8793

**Parent' Charter Unit in the Department for Education**
Sanctuary Buildings
Great Smith Street
London SW1P 3BT
Telephone: 0171 925 6155

## The local government ombudsmen

*For Greater London, Kent, Surrey, East Sussex and West Sussex*
21 Queen Anne's Gate
London SW1H 9BU
Telephone: 0171 915 3210

*For East Anglia, The South, The South-West, The West and Central England*
The Oaks
Westwood Way
Westwood Business Park
Coventry CV4 8JB
Telephone: 01203 695999

*For East Midlands and North of England*
Beverley House
17 Shipton Road
York YO3 6FZ
Telephone: 01904 630151

## Services

**Association of Manufacturers of Domestic Appliances (AMDEA)**
Rapier House
40-46 Lamb's Conduit Street
London WC1N 3NW
Telephone: 0171 405 0666

**British Association of Removers**
3 Churchill Court
58 Station Road
North Harrow
Middlesex HA2 7SA
Telephone: 0181 861 3331

**The British Decorators Association**
32 Coton Road
Nuneaton
Warwickshire CV11 5TW
Telephone: 01203 353776

**The British Institute of Professional Phtography**
2 Amwell End
Ware
Herts SG12 9HN
Telephone: 01920 464011

**British Leather Confederation**
Kings Park Road
Moulton Park
Northampton NN3 6JD
Telephone: 01604 494131

**The British Photographic Association**
Ambassador House
Bridstock Road
Thornton Heath
Surrey CR7 7JG
Telephone: 0181 665 5395

**British Textile Technology Group**
Wira House
West Park Ring Road
Leeds LS16 6QL
Telephone: 01532 591999

**Chartered Institute of Building**
Englemere
Kings Ride
Ascot
Berkshire SL5 8BJ
Telephone: 01344 23355

**Domestic Appliance Service Association**
Hazeldene
Wengeo Lane
Ware
Herts SG12 0EG
Telephone: 01920 465928

**Dry-cleaning Technology Centre**
8 Wells Promenade
Ilkley
West Yorkshire LS29 9LF
Telephone: 01943 816545

**Fabric Care Research Association**
Forest House Laboratories
Knaresborough Road
Harrogate
North Yorkshire HG2 7LZ
Telephone: 01423 885977

**General Dental Council**
37 Wimpole Street
London W1M 8DQ
Telephone: 0171 486 2171

**General Medical Council**
44 Hallam Street
London W1N 6AE
Telephone: 0171 580 7642

**General Optical Council**
41 Harley Sreet
London W1N 2DJ
Telephone: 0171 580 3898

**Glass and Glazing Federation**
44-48 Borough High Street
London SE1 1XB
Telephone: 0171 403 7177

**Hairdressers Council**
12 David House
45 High Street
London SE25 6HJ
Telephone: 0181 771 6205

**Heating and Ventilating
Contractors Association**
Esca House
34 Palace Court
Bayswater
London W2 4JG
Telephone: 0171 229 2488

**Incorporated Society of
Valuers and
Auctioneers**
3 Cadogan Gate
London SW1X 0AS
Telephone: 0171 235 2282

**Institute of Plumbing**
64 Station Lane
Hornchurch
Essex RM12 6NB
Telephone: 01708 472791

**The Institute of Photographic
Apparatus and Repair
Technicians**
228 Regent's Park Road
London N3 3HP
Telephone: 0181 346 8302

**Institute of Trichologists**
228 Stockwell Road
London SW9 9SU
Telephone: 0171 733 2056

**Institution of Structural
Engineers**
11 Upper Belgrave Street
London SW1X 8BH
Telephone: 0171 235 4535

**Kitchen Specialists
Association (KSA)**
PO Box 311
Worcester WR1 1DN
Telephone: 01905 726066

**The Master Photographers'
Association**
97 East Street
Epsom
Surrey KT17 1EA
Telephone: 01372 726123

**National Association of Estate
Agents**
Arbon House
21 Jury Street
Warwick CV34 4EH
Telephone: 01926 496800

**National Association of
Funeral Directors**
618 Warwick Road
Solihull
West Midlands B91 1AA
Telephone: 0121 711 1343

**National Association of
Launderette Industries**
79 Glen Eyre Road
Southampton
SO2 3NN
Telephone: 01703 766328

**National Association of
Plumbing, Heating and
Mechanical Services
Contractors**
14/15 Ensign Business Centre
Westwood Business Park
Westwood Way
Coventry CV4 8JA
Telephone: 01203 470626

**National Childminding
Association**
8 Masons Hill
Bromley
Kent BT2 9EY
Telephone: 0181 466 0200
(only on Mon/Tues 2–4 pm
and Thurs 1—3 pm)

**National Federation of
Painting and
Decorating**
82 New Cavendish Street
London W1M 8AD
Telephone: 0171 580 5588

**National Hairdressers'
Federation**
11 Goldington Road
Bedford MK40 3JY
Telephone: 01234 360332

**Complaints about NHS
Services**
*For England*
11th Floor, Millbank Tower
Millbank
London SW1P 3QP
Telephone: 0171 276 2035

*For Scotland*
Ground Floor
1 Atholl Place
Edinburgh EH3 8HP
Telephone: 0131 225 7465

*For Wales*
4th Floor Pearl Assurance
House
Greyfriars Road
Cardiff CF1 3AG
Telephone: 01222 394621

*For Northern Ireland*
The Ombudsman
Freepost
Belfast BT1 6BR
Telephone: 01232
233832/0800 282036

**The National Pharmaceutical
Association**
38-42 St Peter's Street
St Albans
Herts AL1 3NP
Telephone: 01727 832161

**OFFER**
Hagley House
Hagley Road
Birmingham B16 8QG
Telephone: 0121 456 2100

**OFGAS**
Stockley House
130 Wilton Road
London SW1V 1LQ
Telephone: 0171 828 0898

**OFTEL**
50 Ludgate Hill
London EC4M 7JJ
Telephone: 0171 634 8700

**OFWAT**
Centre City Tower
7 Hill Street
Birmingham B5 4UA
Telephone: 0121 625 1300

**Ombudsman for the
Corporate Estate
Agents Co Ltd**
PO Box 1114
4 Bridge Street
Salisbury
Wiltshire SP1 14Q
Telephone: 01722 333306

**Parcelforce**
Freepost
Solaris Court
Davy Avenue
Milton Keynes MK5 8PP

**Post Office Counters Ltd**
Freepost
St Albans
Herts AL1 5BR

**POUNC**
*For England*
6 Hercules Road
London SE1 7DN
Telephone: 0171 928 9458

**POUNC**
*For Northern Ireland*
7th Floor
Chamber of Commerce House
22 Great Victoria Street
Belfast BT2 7PU
Telephone: 01232 244113

**POUNC**
*For Scotland*
2 Greenside Lane
Edinburgh EH1 3AH
Telephone: 0131 244 5576

**POUNC**
*For Wales*
1st Floor, Caradog House
St Andrews Place
Cardiff CF1 3BE
Telephone: 01222 374028

**Retail Motor Industry
Federation**
201 Great Portland Street
London W1N 6AB
Telephone: 0171 580 9122

**Royal Institute of British
Architects**
66 Portland Place
London W1N 4AD
Telephone: 0171 580 5533

**Royal Institution of
Chartered Surveyors**
12 Great George Street
Parliament Square
London SW1P 3AD
Telephone: 0171 222 7000

**Scot Innovation and
Development**
Netherdale
Galashiels
Selkirkshire TD1 3EY
Telephone: 01896 752196

**Scottish Motor Traders
Association**
3 Palmerston Place
Edinburgh EH12 5AF
Telephone: 0131 225 3643

**Society of Motor
Manufacturers and
Traders Limited**
Forbes House
Halkin Street
London SW1X 7DS
Telephone: 0171 235 7000

**Textile Services Association
Ltd**
7 Churchill Court
58 Station Road
North Harrow
Middlesex HA2 7SA
Telephone: 0181 863 7755

# Chapter 4

# Holidays and Travel

## CHOOSING A HOLIDAY

When you're booking a holiday you are booking a dream... hot sun, deserted beaches, powder snow, utter peace. Whatever you are looking for, the more questions you ask the more likely you are to find it.

Brochures must not mislead the public (the Trade Descriptions Act makes it a criminal offence) but it is the nature of advertising to glorify reality, and the nature of the holiday-maker to fantasise – about 30 per cent of complaints made to Trading Standards about holidays are about brochure descriptions. A brochure will always show the resort's best side; there may not be a bad side but ask some questions to find out. You have rights but getting your money back will never make up for the disappointment of a ruined break.

### Your options

It is a common misconception that travel agents are independent and will give you impartial advice; in practice, 'directional selling' is rife and you may only be told about the holidays of a linked tour operator. The Office of Fair Trading investigated integrated travel firms in 1994 and concluded that there is still a 'wide choice of competitively priced packages available

---

### Who Owns Who

The three big tour operators, Thomson, Airtours and First Choice, each own their own airlines and travel agents (Lunn Poly and Britannia; Going Places and Thomas Cook respectively).

---

### Surcharges

Ask if you may be subject to surcharges. Tour operators can charge you extra ('a surcharge') if it is stated in the brochure. ABTA members must explain what the charge is for, and place any surcharges over 30 days before you set off. If the surcharge amounts to more than 10 per cent of the total price then ABTA members must give you the chance to cancel and get a full refund. There are time limits for this, so you have to act quickly.

---

to holiday-makers' – but you may have to shop around to find them.

When you see a holiday you like, try to get an unbiased view of the resort by asking questions. Take a look at travel guides, travel programmes and travel magazines, and get personal recommendations where possible. Every travel agent should also have a copy of the *Hotel Gazetteer*, which gives unbiased descriptions of all hotels – ask to have a look.

### Hidden costs

Look for 'hidden costs' before you sign. Read the booking conditions – these contain details about your contract that are legally binding.

Ask whether you have to pay extra for:
- the journey (daytime or weekend flights, airport taxes, transfers)
- the hotel (full board, a single room, balcony/view/special room, private toilet/shower/bath)
- children (are other companies offering free or reduced child places?)
- excursions or other extras (very few tour operators charge surcharges – but it is still worth asking).

### Vital questions

Asking lots of questions about the holiday has two benefits; first, you will know what you are getting, and, secondly, you will be aware of the terms and conditions of the contract you are agreeing to. Once you have signed the booking form you have accepted the contract – which may oblige you to pay increased holiday charges, accept changes in flight times and even go to a different (but similar) resort.

---

**Extras**

Some holidays, such as 18-30s, charge a competitive base rate but hard-sell 'excursions', parties and nights-out once you arrive. These can end up costing in total as much as the original package.

Resort reps are paid commission on the basis of the excursions that they sell. It is their job to make you feel that unless you take a sardine & sangria trip into the bay or ride camels at dusk, you will not have had 'the full experience'. Some reps are very persuasive sellers.

- Be aware that you are being manipulated – phrases such as 'places are limited' are designed to get your cheque book out.
- Do not book unless you really want to go.
- Bear in mind that it may be cheaper if you book the trip independently using local transport and guides.

---

## About the journey:

- What will I be entitled to if the flight is delayed or overbooked?
- When should I confirm?
- What are the booking conditions?
- What rights does the company have to change flight times without compensation or warning?
- If you are taking a connecting flight, will the company take responsibility for delays that cause you to miss it?

## About the hotel:

- How far is the hotel from the amenities/beach? Ask for walking distance in kilometres by path/road. People commonly accept vague assurances such as 'it's only ten minutes away' or 'you can see on the map it's not far' and then find the situation is different when they arrive. Travel agents may not know the answers to your questions but press them to find out.
- Does it have a lift/wheelchair access/childcare facilities *on site* ?
- What *exactly* do 'children's facilities' refer to? Possibly no more than 'special mealtimes' and 'games' (when there is sufficient demand). Are

there babysitters? How much do they cost? Do not give the brochure the benefit of the doubt – a decrepit tennis table in a musty cellar could be billed as 'a children's games room'.

- Can special meal requests be met? (*See* Special requests, page 114)

## About the resort:

- How far is the beach from the hotel? Are there trained lifeguards? Is the beach suitable for swimming/wind-surfing/children?
- Are the beaches free? Do you have to pay for umbrellas, chairs, etc?
- Are there jellyfish or other hazards which you ought to avoid?
- What is the weather like at the time you are going? It's easy to think that 'Thailand's hot' but how hot?

## Trade associations

The holiday market is highly competitive, and even well-established firms can go under in a bad season, as recent casualties have shown. If you book with a member of one of the trade associations shown here, you can be sure that, in the event of bankruptcy, your money will be refunded if you have not taken your holiday, or you will be brought home if you are on holiday.

---

### ABTA (Association of British Travel Agents)

ABTA represents most of the country's well-known tour operators and travel agents. All members agree to abide by a Code of Conduct, which is designed to protect the consumer from the more common causes of spoilt package holidays.

- Members are bonded.
- If ABTA agents pass on price increases of more than 10 per cent, you are entitled to your money back. The price of your holiday cannot increase within 30 days of departure.
- Agents ensure that your requirements (such as vegetarian meals) are effectively relayed to the tour operator.
- Low-cost independent arbitration service.
- Members agree to address written complaints within 28 days, to speed up the resolution of problems.

**ABTA**

---

**AITO (Association of Independent Tour Operators)**

AITO members tend to be the smaller, specialist companies – independent tour operators rather than the package holiday giants. All members agree to a Quality Charter and Code of Business Conduct.

- AITO members are fully bonded.
- AITO runs a low-cost Independent Dispute Settlement Service

**AITO**
THE ASSOCIATION
OF INDEPENDENT
TOUR OPERATORS

---

The Package Travel Regulations, which were brought in in 1993, state that all travel firms must provide their customers with financial security. They can do it in one of three ways – through bonding (in partnership with trade associations), insurance policy or trust account.

Trade associations do a lot more than just give financial security. They set down codes of conduct for their members which can be useful in establishing how you are treated where the law is vague. For example, if you book with an ABTA (Association of British Travel Agents) member you do not have to accept increases in the price of your holiday of over 10 per cent, whereas with other firms you may be contractually obliged to fork out more than this.

One of the most reassuring aspects of these trade associations is the arbitration or dispute settlement service which they run for their members. If you have a problem with an ABTA member which is not sorted out on holiday, you can be sure that ABTA will address that complaint within 28 days of your writing to them. If you cannot reach a settlement, you can turn to the low-cost arbitration service for help.

### Buying a package holiday
Before you book make sure that your tour operator or travel agent is a member of ABTA and/or AITO and that the tour operator displays an ATOL (Air Travel Organisers' Licence) number if your holiday includes flights.

### Buying a flight only
Independent travel is not as well regulated as package holidays. When you

buy a flight check that the tour operator is covered by the ATOL scheme (the booking confirmation slip will have an ATOL number on it) unless a ticket is issued as soon as you pay.

There is no Government or other scheme to protect against scheduled airline failure. If you book direct with a scheduled airline, it's a good idea to use a credit card. This will give you a claim against your credit card company for any ticket that costs more than £100, if the airline goes bust. But the credit card company won't be liable if your payment is made to an agent – and **debit** cards like Switch don't give the same protection.

### Buying a flight from a bucket shop

If there are unsold tickets on scheduled flights airlines may choose to cut their losses and sell them on at whatever price they can get a few days before departure. These cut-price tickets may be sold through shops known as 'bucket shops', who advertise in the local and national press. Thousands of people have travelled happily and cheaply on tickets bought from bucket shops, but some have been left out of pocket by companies that go out of business or out of circulation. Here's how to minimise the risk:

- Do not buy a discounted ticket unless the company has an ATOL licence or can issue you a ticket at the time you hand over your money.
- Do not buy a scheduled ticket unless the company is registered with IATA (International Air Transport Association) or ABTA.
- Do not buy from them if they make you suspicious – intuition is

---

### AUC – Air Transport User's Council

If you have a legitimate claim against a scheduled airline, and have not received a satisfactory response from the airline, the AUC may be able to help. They can take up your case, but cannot enforce their views or act as a formal arbitrator. The types of cases they can be involved in, include:

- passengers denied boarding and offered vouchers rather than cash
- airlines who are taking months to pay compensation for lost baggage
- passengers attacked by drunks in flight, and not given support by the airline

---

### ATOL (Air Travel Organisers' Licence)

Any business selling air holidays or scheduled flights where a ticket
cannot be issued straightaway must have an ATOL licence.  Look for an
ATOL number when you book, and check that it is valid with the CAA.

• The scheme protects you from losing money or being stranded abroad if
the company goes bust.

• Travel agents can act on behalf of ATOL holders - ask which one your
booking is with.

Confirmation: an ATOL holder must send you a confirmation of contract
within 7 days of receiving your travel booking, and the travel agent must
pass it on to you.

---

sometimes the only sign that you may have of a disreputable trader.

• Pay by credit card if possible. You have extra protection if the
company goes bust or there are problems with your holiday – as long
as the cost of the holiday is more than £100 per person. When you
complain you should go to whoever you paid, but you can hold the
credit card company responsible if they do not sort it out.

• Check with the airline before you go that your seat is confirmed and
paid for on the flight the shop says.

**Is it a schedule or charter flight?**  The only sure way of knowing what
type of flight you are booking is to ask. You have different rights
depending on which flight you buy.

### Scheduled tickets

• are offered by airlines, and fly at regular times the year round

• are sold by travel agents acting as agents for the airline or ATOL
holders. If you book direct with the airline you have no protection if
the airline goes bust.

• can be more flexible than charter flights. Check the booking
conditions to see the constraints on changing your flight time.

• are recognisable by the range of tickets available – APEX, Youth and

Business class tickets are usually offered on scheduled flights, whereas charter flights normally have only one class.

## Charter flights

- are bought by a holiday company and sold on to you – so if you buy a charter flight your contract is with the holiday company. If the selling agent has an ATOL licence, you will be given a refund or flight home if the agent goes bust.
- are bought on a 'Use it or Lose it' basis – it is rarely possible for you to change the time of a charter flight.
- can be re-scheduled by the holiday company – if a flight is half-empty they can cancel it and put passengers on to the next flight. (Booking conditions will tell you what you are entitled to if this happens.)

## Protection on activity holidays

If you are booking an activity holiday you'll need more than financial protection; you'll want to know that the activity centre you are booking with is competent and takes reasonable safety precautions.

In recent years tragedies such as the Lyme Bay canoe disaster in March 1993, where four schoolchildren drowned on an outdoor activity course, have highlighted the need for better regulation of activity holidays. At the time of going to print a bill calling for a clampdown on under-18 activity centres is being heard, but no safety standards have yet been set in place.

The British Activity Holiday Association (BAHA) will be able to give advice. Ring 01932-252994 for details.

---

**Tip**

Logos signal membership but it is worth calling to check. Brochures are often 18 months old – the company may have stopped being a member of the trade association or no longer hold a licence by the time you make your booking.

---

### No such thing as a free holiday

'Free holidays' are sometimes used to promote other goods and services. You may be told that you have won a 'free holiday' or 'holiday prize' – but look into the real costs involved. In some cases 'winners' actually end up paying more for their 'holiday prize' than they would have done if they had booked it all themselves.

- Never pay any money until you know *all* the terms and conditions of the holiday.
- Compare the offer with the price of a similar package tour to the same destination.

---

## YOUR RIGHTS

Your rights when you book a holiday come from three sources: the law, the trade associations the travel agent or tour operator is a member of, and the booking conditions the travel agent or tour operator sets itself.

**1** The **law** gives you basic rights.

**2 Trade associations** add to these rights, by setting codes of conduct for their members. Codes of conduct are not legally enforceable but are rarely violated. Most trade associations run arbitration or dispute settlement schemes to help resolve any disputes. The trade associations to look for when you book are listed on pages 103–104.

**3 Booking conditions** are the final layer of consumer rights. Many companies offer higher standards of customer service than the minimum standards set down by law and trade associations, and their statement of these will be found on your booking form or the inside cover of your ticket. Booking conditions form part of your contract with a company and are legally binding. They will usually state cancellation and compensation terms, and set limits on their rights to pass on price increases as a result of factors like changes in the exchange rate.

Although holidays are normally booked through a travel agent (for example, Thomas Cook, Going Places, Lunn Poly), your contract is with the tour organisers, whose name features on brochures (such as First Choice, Airtours, Thomson).

Your rights in the most common situations, such as unsatisfactory accommodation or delayed flights, are detailed below.

## Misleading brochures

Anything that is said about goods or services by the seller amounts to a trade description and, by law, must not be false. If the tour operator tells you that the beach is a ten-minute walk away or there are facilities for children, then legally you have a right to expect these. It will make it easier if you have any vital descriptions in writing. *However*, the travel agent or tour operator cannot be held liable for diversions from their descriptions that they cannot control, could not reasonably be expected to predict or have known about from their local knowledge.

For example, if you arrive at your hotel to find that the surrounding area is undergoing major civil engineering work then your entitlement varies. If the work has been underway for some time, the tour operator should have informed you over two weeks before you left and given you the opportunity of an exchange. If it was unforeseeable – an emergency response to flooding or an earthquake, say – then the tour operator does not have to refund any money.

Reps in the area should keep tour operators informed of events that will affect your holiday – such as the cessation of bus services to the beach, or the start of building works nearby – and they should tell you immediately. If local circumstances affect your holiday substantially you will be entitled to a refund or change of destination.

## Imposed surcharges

Tour operators cannot pass on all increased costs in package holidays. The

---

### Brochure vs adverts

Anything said in a brochure amounts to a trade description. Brochures should give comprehensive descriptions of the components of a package. Newspaper ads are not considered to be part of a holiday 'brochure' and you could not usually use an advert in a case against a tour operator.

first 2 per cent of any increases must be absorbed by the tour operator, and no price increase may be passed on within 30 days of departure. The law says that if a price increase is 'significant' the consumer may withdraw from a contract without penalty. 'Significant' is open to interpretation – if it amounts to 10 per cent of the total price (the maximum that ABTA allows) you may have a case. Ask Trading Standards or a covering trade association.

Conferences and incentive travel can be subject to changes until a very late stage, and are generally exempt from the restrictions above: in these cases the price changes *can* be passed on to you.

### Unreasonable accommodation

Tour operators have a legal obligation to supply accommodation of a 'reasonable' standard. What is considered reasonable will depend on what you pay and how many stars the accommodation has, but you can expect basics such as a reasonable standard of cleanliness.

### Problems with a travel agent or tour operator

Tour operators and travel agents, like all service providers, are expected to use 'reasonable care and skill' when booking a holiday for you. If they are negligent or do not fulfil this legal obligation, they are liable and you may be entitled to a refund or damages. If you book two tickets to the World Cup with accommodation, you can reasonably expect the tour operator to fulfil their duty. If two months later they ring to say they can't find flights and the tickets are sold out, you have a case against them. Ask for your money back and damages for loss of enjoyment.

### Force majeure

Legally, tour operators and airlines are not responsible for any alterations to your holiday caused by 'force majeure' such as a war, riot, civil strife or earthquake, and do not have to compensate you for the loss of the whole, or any part, of your holiday.

However, tour operators may choose to compensate you. For example, when in the summer of 1994, the Foreign Office advised all British nationals not to visit the Gambia because of a coup, tour operators offered exchange holidays or money back to all holiday-makers affected.

## Alterations to your holiday

If a tour operator needs to make significant alterations to your holiday they should tell you without significant delay. Legally you are entitled to either accept the change (which must not alter the standard of your holiday), or receive a prompt refund. (This does not cover flights that are delayed due to factors beyond the operator's control such as bad weather.) What counts as 'significant' is arguable. Typically, a change of hotel or resort, or flight changes of over 12 hours, would be considered significant.

**If the tour operator cancels** If the tour operator cancels before you have paid the full balance you have the choice of accepting an equivalent offer or your money back. You are not obliged to accept an alternative.

If a tour operator cancels your holiday after the balance of the cost is due (which is usually eight to ten weeks before you go), it must be for reasons beyond his control and you are entitled to a refund, which should be paid promptly, and also to compensation.

**If you want to cancel** Your cancellation rights are set out in your booking conditions – cancelling can be expensive.

## Flights and rights

**Alterations** If alterations are made to a scheduled flight, you have no rights at all, beyond those laid out in the booking conditions.

On charter flights, most booking conditions allow 'minor' (up to 12 hours) changes without entitlement to compensation, with an option of a refund for changes of over 12 hours. ABTA members must not make any major changes less than 14 days before your departure – if they do you are entitled to a full refund. Always read the booking conditions before you sign! If the change means that you incur extra expense – because you can no longer get a lift to the airport, for example – accept the change 'under protest'. You may be able to claim compensation.

> ### Remember
>
> Once you sign the booking form, the contract between you and the tour operator becomes legally binding. Read it carefully and ask for advice on anything that you are not sure about.

**Overbooking** Flights are almost always overbooked on the assumption that not all passengers will turn up – if everybody shows then the last to check in may be 'bumped' on to the next flight. EC regulations give you a legal entitlement to 'denied boarding compensation'.

Airlines may offer compensation in the form of vouchers but you do not have to accept these if you prefer cash. European flights delayed less than two hours entitle you to £57.93, long-haul flights delayed by more than four entitle you to £231.75. The airline should also pay the cost of getting a message to your destination.

**Delays** If you are delayed for reasons such as bad weather, airport congestion or industrial action, you have no legal right to compensation. Some airlines and tour operators provide food, drink or overnight accommodation but they are not obliged to. Check booking conditions.

**Missed connections** If you are on a scheduled flight which involves changing to a different airline check the airline's policies on delays when you book – they differ.

### Booking
**Over the phone** Tour organisers must communicate all the terms of the contract to you in writing before the contract is made. If you book by phone, study the brochure, where the terms of the contract are set out.

**Booking at the last minute** Last-minute bookings (ones that have been taken within 14 days of departure) are subject to cancellation charges.

**Transferring a booking** Your right to transfer a booking will be specified in your booking conditions. Transfers are usually limited to specified circumstances such as illness, death of a close relative or jury service, and tour organisers should be notified a minimum of 21 days before departure.

**Tour operators claiming limited liability** Occasionally tour operators make statements of limited liability. These may not survive a legal challenge so do not be put off.

## Lost luggage

Airlines have to pay compensation for lost luggage based on weight ($20 per kilo), not cash value. Most will pay for essentials while they attempt to find your luggage, and deduct this advance from the compensation paid if luggage is lost. Suitable insurance, with new-for-old cover, and cover for expensive items, is recommended. Most policies will also pay you compensation if your luggage is lost for more than 12 hours. Fill in a claim form before leaving the baggage hall and keep copies of all documents.

## Your hotel is overbooked

You should be offered accommodation of an equivalent standard by your tour operator. If it is of a lower standard you should be refunded the difference. If you are not happy with the alternative, complain to the rep and accept 'under protest' – this will enable you to claim compensation at a later date. The facilities available, location and distance from amenities, quality of rooms, and type of hotel are the factors to mention when claiming compensation.

### Cancellation fees

Cancellation fees are meant to reflect the money that the tour operator will lose, and are not designed to be punitive. If you think that you are being charged more than the operator stands to lose, try to renegotiate. Holiday insurance may reimburse cancellation fees in certain circumstances.

Additional expense which you incur as a result of the changes such as child care or car hire, should be compensated by your tour operator. Ask your rep if they can provide payment for this, but make it clear that you may decide to claim more later – accept 'under protest'.

## Special requests

Most booking forms have a section called 'special requests' where you are invited to ask for things like vegetarian meals, sea-views, double beds, etc. Legally these requests do not have to be met. If you fill in the box the tour operator should meet them where possible. There is no way that you can build your requirements into your contract, and there is no way that your travel agent will guarantee the requests although those relating to medical conditions and disability are more likely to be accommodated.

If you chase them up you are more likely to have your requests met..

# HOLIDAY MONEY

When you choose your holiday money, bear two things in mind: usefulness and safety. If you lose your cards or cash or have them stolen, report it immediately to the police and the card issuer. Few insurance companies pay on claims which are not accompanied by a local police report or report number.

## Cash

**Risky:** some travel insurance covers a limited amount of cash, usually between £250 and £500. Avoid carrying too much; $2,000 was stolen from one couple as they brushed their teeth in their en suite bathroom in

---

### Compensation

EC regulations state that cash compensation should always be offered if you are denied boarding. A large number of airlines still offer vouchers as compensation, and do not have the facility to offer cash at the airport. If you want cash, ask how you can exchange the voucher for cash at a later date.

---

### Travel wisdom

Follow these tips to increase your chance of trouble-free travel:

- Buy your holiday insurance when you buy your holiday – then if you have to cancel (eg. due to ill health) you may be covered (check the cancellation terms when you buy).
- Confirm your reservations. On some flights they are not a formality but a necessity and if you do not confirm within the stated time before departure (usually 24 or 48 hours) the company is legally entitled to give your seat to someone else. You may not always be entitled to another flight.

---

Nepal; they had no return tickets or credit cards. Some countries limit the amount you can take in or out; ask your tour operator.

### Travellers' cheques

**Safe:** if they're lost or stolen it's easy to get a quick refund or replacements. **Value:** Travellers' cheques often get a better exchange rate than cash. But you can end up paying commission to buy the cheques and sometimes when you sell them as well.

### Credit cards

**Safe:** if you report stolen cards immediately you will not be liable for fraudulent use. Keep the emergency number for lost and stolen cards with you at all times. It will take some time to get replacement cards, so don't rely on them completely. **Value:** This is often the cheapest way of paying on holiday. You won't pay any extra for using your credit card to make purchases abroad but if you use it for cash you'll either pay a 1.5 per cent commission or daily interest. Check to see whether there is a daily limit on withdrawals. Remember that if you pay for your travellers' cheques on a credit card you can be charged a handling fee of 1.5 per cent.

Credit cards are a safe form of currency when you have them in your possession but what happens when you let them out of your sight? There are cases of duplicate cards being made in restaurants in the time it takes for someone to pay their bill, two copy slips being made (and counter-

---

**Now you see it now you don't**

In an attempt to curb fraudulent card use, some credit card companies watch for 'unusual patterns of usage'. So if you don't use your credit card all year and then start to charge food, rental cars, accomodation and drinks you may find that it is retained or not authorised the next time you come to use it. Ask your credit card company if they do this.

---

signed later) when your card is swapped, and people using your credit card number on the phone to pay for goods. Risks always seem higher when you are abroad and don't know local etiquette. The safest option is not to let your card out of your sight.

## HOLIDAY INSURANCE

Your suitcase has gone missing, your hotel's half-built, your credit card's been stolen and you've got a jellyfish bite that needs treating... it could happen to you, so go prepared.

Many tour operators are now trying to sell holiday insurance alongside the holiday. Don't accept this automatically as some policies leave you under-insured. It is worth shopping around to find a policy that suits your needs. Under their Code of Practice, ABTA agents must tell you about the types of insurance available.

**Do ...**
- Check your other insurance policies first. Household insurance and private medical cover may offer some protection, as do some credit card companies. Some things, such as cancellation, may not be covered.
- Ask to see the policy details before you buy – not just the brochure. Be wary of companies that are not willing to send you the details; it is in breach of the statement of practice from the Association of British Insurers (ABI).
- Read the small print, particularly exclusion details and the conditions under which claims will be allowed. Many policies set an upper limit

on individual items. Insure items over that value separately.

- Insurance may only compensate you when you return to the UK, so make sure that you have adequate provision for an emergency. If you have to pay out money abroad make sure you get and keep receipts.
- Detail valuables in the 'all-risks' part.
- If the firm operates a Helpline, keep this number (together with a copy of your policy) with you.

## Don't ...

- Buy a policy just because it's cheap or easy (ie offered by the tour operator).
- Assume that sports or adventurous activities are covered. If your idea of cliff walking is another person's idea of rock climbing without the ropes, will you be covered?
- Forget the excess.
- Assume all items are covered – high-value and high-risk items (personal stereos, camcorders, cameras) are sometimes excluded.
- Mistake 'free' travel insurance with credit cards for proper travel insurance – it may not be comprehensive.

## Minimum cover

Cover for medical expenses, loss of belongings, cancellation and personal liability should be thought of as a basic minimum.

**Medical expenses** Look for medical expenses plus a lump sum if you are injured, disabled or killed. Minimum cover of £250,000 in Europe and £1 million in the US and the rest of the world is recommended.

Some countries, such as EC countries and Australia, have a reciprocal agreement with Britain which reduces some medical treatment costs if you are employed or receiving benefits (but not if you are 'non-employed', such as a housewife). Details are in leaflet T4, 'Health advice for travellers', available from any post office. Additional insurance cover is recommended – you may need to be flown home or have a relative flown out to visit you if your illness or injuries are severe.

Some companies will not pay for treatment related to pre-existing illnesses (such as asthma) or advanced pregnancies.

You generally have to pay extra for sports cover – so if you are windsurfing, skiing or hang-gliding a standard policy may be no good.

**Cancellation** Approximately half of all travel insurance claims are for cancellations. Look for cover that will meet the full cost of your holiday. Check the terms: some insist on a notice period in order for you to get all your money back. Look for policies that cover you in the event of compulsory redundancy, illness, the death or illness of a close relative or business associate, damage to your home by flood, fire or storm, or being called for jury service or as a witness. Cover is usually £3–5,000, policies that offer less (£1,500, for example) may not cover your losses completely.

**Personal liability** Accidents – such as causing damage to someone or something – can be horrendously expensive, especially in the litigation-happy United States. Minimum cover of £1m is recommended for everywhere but the United States, where £2m should be your minimum.

**Loss of belongings** If you have an 'all risks' policy, your home contents insurance may cover your belongings abroad – check before you buy. If not, look for a value comparable to the value of your belongings (some companies offer quite small amounts) and make sure that you itemise any valuables. It is usually possibly to cover cameras but most standard policies will not pay out enough to cover the loss of expensive jewellery (a usual maximum payout £1,500). Also, check the conditions under which you can claim. Sometimes you need a receipt to prove their worth and a police report if you have specified them. Most policies allow up to £100 for the purchase of essentials if your baggage is delayed. Loss of passport/money.

**Other checks** Missed departure or delay – some will only cover you for the first delay – if you have two flights this may not help.

## WHILE YOU ARE AWAY

Take all the relevant booking documents with you when you go – you may need them if things go wrong. If you have the brochure, booking contract and insurance forms with you, you can be sure of what you were promised and what you are entitled to. If something goes wrong, it is the tour operator who must sort it out for you.

### Credit card cover

Paying by credit card gives you extra protection if the holiday costs more than £100. (Debit cards and charge cards do not offer this facility.) Initially try to reach an agreement with your tour operator. If this fails, or the tour operator or travel agent goes out of business, contact your credit card company who is equally liable. NEVER quote your credit card number over the telephone unless you are making a firm booking.

## Package holidays

- Take action immediately: complain to the tour rep to give them the chance to put it right. The onus is on you. If you do not give the provider a chance to correct their mistakes, you are unlikely to win a later case for compensation. Ask clearly for what you want.
- Contact your tour operator at home and ask them to sort it out if you are not happy with the action your rep is taking.
- Collect evidence. Keep a diary of events and a record of the names, times and content of any relevant conversations. Take photographs of what is wrong. Take names and addresses of other holiday-makers who are aware of the problem. Keep receipts for any extra bills. Complain in writing to your travel agent or tour operator. Tell the company what went wrong and send them any facts and photographs you have. State the amount of compensation you want.
- Take further action if your complaint is still not sorted out. If the tour operator is not offering adequate compensation or you are not happy with the response you are getting to your complaint, then you can take action through the courts or an independent arbitration scheme. Contact the trade association for advice on how to proceed. If you do not want to use their arbitration service you can consider taking the tour operator to court, to be tried under civil law. You cannot do both. Think about using the small claims procedure.

## Independent travellers

If you have booked hotels, tickets and cruises yourself while you are abroad, then the best thing to do is try to resolve the situation on the spot if things to wrong. If the matter is serious, a British Consulate may be able to help. Taking any claim further will be very difficult once you leave the country but it is possible. If you have to take the service provider to court, it will probably be in the host country's court, in which case a solicitor familiar with the law can help you. Contact the Law Society (0171 242 1222).

### On-the-spot compensation
This may undermine your right to full compensation at a later date. Do not sign anything stating that you accept this as a full and final settlement of any claims – you do not know what will happen next. If your rep has to give you on-the-spot payments – to cover the cost of car hire after moving you to an out-of-town resort, for example – put it in writing that you are accepting 'under protest' and then you will be able to claim at a later date.

**Calculating compensation** Compensation may take account of disappointment and inconvenience as well as monetary loss.

Break the cost of your holiday down into components:

| | |
|---|---|
| Accommodation (full board) | £250 |
| Airport tax and transfers | £ 25 |
| Flight | £125 |
| Limitless water sports | £100 |
| **Total cost** | **£500** |

If water sports weren't available, try claiming £100, the value of the watersports, plus £x for loss of enjoyment, or your expenses if you paid someone else for water sports while you were there.

Be reasonable when making out-of-pocket expenses. For example, if your baggage is lost and you have to make emergency purchases, these should be for essentials such as underwear and basic clothing, not designer cocktail dresses for pre-dinner drinks.

### Hiring a car abroad
Take your driving licence with you if you want to rent a car. Check the

---

### Letters of complaint

Keep letters of complaint short and to the point, stating:

- the bare facts - your name, holiday dates, hotel, booking reference
- the complaint – give a chronological account of your complaints, with dates, times and people involved. There may have been a whole host of annoyances which were aggravating but do not warrant compensation – avoid the urge to moan where this will confuse the issue
- the breach committed (if you know what it is) – state the law, code of conduct or booking condition violated
- the evidence available
- the compensation claimed

---

details of the insurance policy cover when you rent. The statutory age limits for driving vary from country to country – if you are in doubt call the national tourist board of the country you are visiting. Some car hire companies impose their own age limits.

**If you pre-book a hire car in the UK** and are not satisfied with it when you arrive, ask for an alternative. If you book through a multi-national company your rights are more likely to be observed (you are entitled to a refund if you are not offered a satisfactory alternative). If you book with a broker then your contract is with the local company, not them. However, if you are not offered a satisfactory vehicle it is worth asking them to help you sort it out.

## Phoning home

Hotels can mark-up phone charges as they like. The Industrial Research Bureau looked into the average percentage mark-ups from the top hotel chains in Europe and found the following: UK 858%, Spain 805%, US 253%, Italy 246%, France 170%.

You can call home from abroad with a BT Chargecard and your call will be charged to your home phone bill. Only use BT chargecards for calls to the UK. Calls made within a foreign country (from Rome to Milan, for example) are routed via the UK and will cost you far more than a coin call.

Hotels can still add a connection charge to your bill if you are using a chargecard. If you make a call through an operator, a charge is added, but calls from some countries (Australia, France, Japan, etc) can be made direct.

The cheapest – but not easiest – option is to make the call from a phone box armed with coins or on a meter and pay afterwards (this service is sometimes offered close to foreign exchange bureaux). Again, check the price.

# OTHER TRAVEL

### Rail travel

The Passengers' Charter has afforded the customer some rights on all lines across Britain – whether franchised or not. You will have to ask in order to get what you are entitled to.

• If your train is delayed by more than an hour you may be entitled to a refund of at least 20 per cent. If the heating breaks down or the buffet car is absent, you will probably be refunded more.

• If your train is delayed by more than an hour and there is a buffet car on board you are entitled to free refreshments as long as stocks last.

• If you reserve a seat and it is not provided, your reservation fee will automatically be refunded. If you buy a ticket and the service is affected – by as little as 15 minutes – you have the right to a full refund if you decide not to travel.

• Season ticket holders are granted additional rights. Each individual group of routes sets certain performance targets for reliability (the number of trains running on time) and those running punctually. If a group fails to reach its targets on a rolling basis over peak-hour services (7 am–10 am, 4 pm–7 pm) season ticket holders are entitled to a 5 per cent discount on their next season ticket. You may be entitled to this discount without ever being late yourself if other trains on your line are persistently delayed. The system may seem a little rigged – it's up to areas to set their own targets after all – but nine out of the 50 areas were giving these service discounts in 1995. (No compensation is given for 'consequent loss', ie. if you miss a deal or a flight as a result of the train delays.)

• In addition to these rights, the railways may, at their discretion, give a refund on tickets where you decide not to travel. Your chances are higher if you make this decision within a few minutes of purchase. If the ticket has been issued in advance, a refund may be given minus an administrative charge. If you have had time to travel to your destination and back by the time you return to the ticket office, you are unlikely to be successful.

• If you bought your ticket from someone who had chartered a train – a football club, for example – it is up to them to define your rights.

**Rail Users' Consultative Committee (RUCC)** If you are not happy with the way that your complaint is being treated by the rail company, contact your regional RUCC (see the telephone directory). Their action depends on the merits of each case; if they think it is a serious case such as a missed connection or stolen luggage, they will take it up with the rail company.

## Coaches and buses

If you are involved in an accident because of a fault of the coach or bus company – such as reckless driving or unroadworthiness – then you may be able to sue for compensation. The only rights you have to compensation in the event of the bus being cold or your journey slow will be stated in the booking conditions on your ticket. If you have a complaint about anything go to the bus or coach company first. If you are unhappy with the action that they take, contact the Traffic Commissioner in the area.

## Ferries

Ferries are the most dangerous form of public transport you can take in terms of risk of fatality. Any ferry that docks on British shores has to be certified as safe by the Marine Safety Agency, and is inspected about once a year. Beyond this, minimum safety standards are set by the country to which the ferry is 'flagged'. Ferries can go to any country to be 'flagged'. Stena Sealink flags its ships in the Bahamas, where standards are lower than in the UK (which has introduced new stability standards, Solas 90, after the *Herald of Free Enterprise* disaster).

If you have problems, complain to the ferry company but to the flag state, and then to the Marine Safety Agency about safety standards.

# USEFUL ADDRESSES

**Advertising Standards
Authority**
Brook House
2-16 Torrington Place
London WC1E 7HN
Telephone: 0171 580 5555
(NB: Report any instances of
misleading brochures or false
advertising claims to the ASA.
They will investigate the
complaint and may withdraw
the brochure.)

**Air Transport Users
Committee (AUC)**
5th Floor, Kingsway House
103 Kingsway
London WC2B 6QX
Telephone: 0171 242 3882

**Association of British Insurers**
51 Gresham Street
London EC2V 7HQ
(NB: Provides *Holiday
Insurance & Motoring Abroad*,
a consumer information sheet;
available with an SAE from:
Consumer Information Sheets
– Holiday.)

**Association of British Travel
Agents (ABTA)**
55-57 Newman Street
London W1P 4AH
Telephone: 0171 637 2444

**Association of Independent
Tour Operators (AITO)**
133a St Margaret's Road
Twickenham
Middlesex TW1 1RG
Telephone: 0181 744 9280

**ATOL (Air Travel Organisers'
Licence) section**
Civil Aviation Authority
(CAA)
45-49 Kingsway
London WC2B 6TE
Telephone: 0171 832 5620

**British Activity Holiday
Association Ltd (BAHA)**
22 Green Lane
Hersham
Walton-on-Thames
Surrey KT12 5TD
Telephone: 01932 252994

**Central Rail Users'
Consultative Committee**
Golden Cross House
8 Duncannon Street
London WC2N 4JT
Telephone: 0171 839
7338/930 1304

**Department of Transport**
2 Marsham Street
London SW1P 3EB
Telephone: 0171 276 3000

**Marine Safety Agency**
Spring Place
105 Commercial Road
Southampton
Surrey SO15 1EG
Telephone: 01703 329100

# Chapter 5

# Finance

Financial products and services are increasingly complicated these days, and when something goes wrong it can be baffling to know where to go for help or redress. Specific advice is given in the following sections, but a general rule, as with so many other consumer problems, is to try and sort it out internally with the branch, office or outlet you dealt with originally, before asking one of the Ombudsmen to investigate and arbitrate. Ombudsmen are Government-appointed consumer 'watchdogs' whose job is to investigate complaints by private individuals against private or public organisations or companies.

## YOUR FINANCIAL RIGHTS

### Plastic cards

There are a variety of 'plastic' cards available to pay for goods and services, or to withdraw cashs.

Card issuers have certain responsibilities about issuing cards to customers, such as only issuing them if they have been requested in writing, or if they are to replace or renew cards that have already been issued. They have to ensure that a PIN (Personal Identification Number) is sent out separately from the card, and given only to the card owner.

### Customers' Responsibilities

- Keep the PIN number secret as far as possible. Destroy any PIN notification when you have received it and don't write it down.
- Keep your card in a safe place.
- Never let anyone else use your card and PIN Number.
- If you lose your card, or it is stolen, or you find someone else has discovered your PIN number, tell the card issuer as soon as possible.

**Liability for loss** If your card is stolen and misused before it reaches you, or while it is in your possession, then the card issuer will normally bear any losses incurred. However, if you have failed to notify them of the loss of the card as soon as reasonably practicable, then you may be liable for the first £50 (maximum) of any misuse. If there is a dispute about liability, it is up to the card issuer to prove that a customer has acted fraudulently or negligently.

## Cheques

Under the Cheques Act, cheques can only be credited to the account of the person or organisation whose name is on the cheque. Banks have no authority to put a cheque into another bank account without consulting the customer in advance.

## Direct debits

Direct debit arrangements are set up by an originating company (such as British Gas, or the Water Board) using your authorisation for regular withdrawals to be made to them from your bank. It is their responsibility to notify you in advance of any changes. If you wish to cancel a direct debit, you should notify the originating company as well as the bank.

## Bank charges

Under the Code of Banking Practice, from 31 December 1996 the main banks and building societies will give at least 14 days' notice of charges that will be deducted as a result of interest and other costs incurred during the charging period. There have been problems in the past where

---

### Unauthorised cash withdrawals

Customers have the same responsibility for looking after their cash cards as they do for any other cards, and the same position regarding liability for unauthorised withdrawals. However, if a loss was due to a fault in the machine or system, then the bank should bear the whole loss. It is up to the bank or building society to prove that the customer is liable.

unexpected charges have led to 'charges on charges', and the new facility is intended to help prevent this happening. Many banks and building societies have introduced 'pre-notification of charges' already.

## COMPLAINING ABOUT FINANCIAL SERVICES

It is important to prepare your complaint carefully. Like all customer complaints, unless your problem is a simple one, put it in writing, and take photocopies. Keep a record of phone calls and meetings, and a note of the names of people you talk to. Don't delay in pursuing your complaint – take action as soon as you know you have a problem.

When you write:
- State the nature of the complaint. Give the name and type of product in question, the policy and reference numbers, the date it was taken out, and the name of the salesman concerned (where an insurance or investment product is involved), your account number and branch name and address, as applicable.
- Give contact details, including a daytime telephone number.
- Give a deadline for a response – but be reasonable. If you are querying the sale of an investment product going back ten years, you cannot expect a full investigation within a week.
- Ask for an acknowledgement.

### Banking complaints

If you have a problem to do with incorrect charging, failure to carry out your instructions, maladminstration, or cash withdrawals, and you believe the bank or building society is at fault, then you should:

1 Contact your branch in person, by telephone or, preferably, in writing. Often the problem, if it is a simple one, can be resolved at once. If it is more difficult, ask the manager to investigate and to respond by letter within a reasonable period of time, say two weeks.

2 If you are still not satisfied, write to the Regional Office

3 If that does not bring results, write to the Head Office's Customer Relations Department.

**4**  If internal negotiations fail contact the Banking Ombudsman (for a complaint against a bank). They can deal with complaints about all kinds of banking business. You must go through the internal complaints procedure first before approaching the Ombudsman.

**5**  Alternatively, contact the Building Societies' Ombudsman for complaints against building societies.

Other sources of advice are:

- The British Bankers' Association
- The Building Societies' Association
- The Council of Mortgage Lenders

## Insurance, investment and pensions complaints

These products can be complex and expensive, and it can be difficult to know whether an error has been made, let alone what to do about it. Common problem areas include discovering that you have been sold the wrong product; that you have been advised to change from one plan to another unnecessarily; that bad advice has resulted in financial loss for you; or that the company refuses to accept a cancellation.

**1**  If you suspect an error then write to the Compliance Officer at the company that sold the product. (If you are worried about your company pension scheme, write to the trustees of the scheme.) Because these products are complicated, investigations into complaints can take longer than other sorts of complaints. Allow two months for the company to look into it (but make sure you have received an acknowledgement).

**2**  If you've heard nothing in that time, apart from an acknowledgement, write to the **PIA** (Personal Investment Authority) **Ombudsman**. He can investigate any firm registered with PIA, including some aspects of insurance, investment and pension products, share dealing, and portfolio management. The PIA is new, and the role of the PIA adjuster is still a little unclear. Some of his terms of reference overlap with other Ombudsmen, and he may refer the case on to another adjudicator, if it would be more appropriate. This could be:

- the **Investment Ombudsman**, who can investigate most investment-related business, and has jurisdiction over all companies regulated by

IMRO (Investment Managers' Regulatory Organisation). While you could write to him directly without going through PIA, you should only do so after you have approached IMRO to ask them to investigate.

- the **Insurance Ombudsman**, who can investigate complaints relating to general insurance such as motor, buildings, contents, health policies, if the company involved is a member of the Ombudsman scheme. He can deal with cases of maladministration to do with personal pensions, so long as the company is not registered with PIA. The marketing and selling of life policies, and problems of maladministration, are more likely to be dealt with by the PIA Ombudsman.

- the **Pensions Ombudsman**, who can investigate complaints to do with both personal and occupational pensions schemes. However, while he can look at the management of occupational pension schemes, his position regarding the management of personal pension schemes is unclear, since in some cases the Insurance Ombudsman may be involved while the PIA Ombudsman may deal with others. In case of doubt you should check which adjudicator the company is affiliated to, and write to him. He will forward your complaint on if necessary. Inquiries to the Pensions Ombudsman should be preceded by an approach to The Occupational Pensions Advisory Service (OPAS)

3 Other organisations that could help you with advice are:
- the Securities and Investment Board (SIB), which is the chief regulatory body
- the Chartered Institute of Arbitrators (Personal Insurance Arbitration Services)
- the Investors' Compensation Scheme
- the Association of British Insurers

---

### Remember

You have 14 days in which to cancel a life insurance, investment or personal pension plan after you have signed up for it.

- the Association of Investment Trust Companies
- the Association of Unit Trusts and Investment Funds

## Complaints about buying and selling shares

If you have a problem with a stockbroker, try to resolve it with the firm concerned first. If this does not work:
- Write to the Securities and Futures Authority (SFA)
- Write to the PIA Ombudsman
- Approach the Stock Exchange if you feel your problem is to do with members' compliance with its rules, for example, or settlement activity.

## Complaints about the Inland Revenue

If you believe you have paid too much tax, and it is due to an error by the Inland Revenue, some of the amount due may be waived. This will depend on your having given the Inland Revenue accurate returns, on time, and that it was reasonable for you to believe you did not owe the tax.

Any problem to do with your tax affairs should be explored with your local tax office first – write to the person in charge.

If you still feel there is a problem, there is a set of procedures set out in a booklet issued by the Inland Revenue called *Mistakes by the Inland Revenue*, which should be available from your local office and gives information about the services of the Inland Revenue Adjudicator, who can investigate most complaints to do with personal tax matters.

## CONSUMER CREDIT

Common forms of credit are high purchase, credit and charge cards, store cards, finance company loans, mail order catalogues, pawnbrokers and moneylenders. Buying on credit usually means that you will have to pay interest on top of the cash price. The APR (Annual Percentage Rate of Charge) figure which is required by law to be quoted should indicate how expensive the credit is. Avoid credit with a high APR if you can – you may well be able to get a cheaper deal elsewhere.

If you are worried that a credit deal you have been offered is unfair, get advice from the Citizens' Advice Bureau, or contact the local Trading Standards Department or Consumer Protection Department, through your local authority. In Northern Ireland, they come under the Department of Economic Development.

## Credit insurance

Credit insurance, also known as payment protection, may be sold with loans and credit cards, and covers repayments if the borrower becomes unemployed or cannot work through ill-health. It can be very expensive, adding perhaps 65 per cent to the cost of credit. Also, it may not cover you if you took voluntary redundancy or became unemployed soon after taking out the policy. Sometimes it does not provide cover for certain age groups, such as pensioners.

Credit insurance is not compulsory, but some lenders add it to your account automatically. Check the small print of any written agreement.

## Cancellation rights

If you decide you want to cancel a credit deal, check the written credit agreement to see what your cancellation rights are. Normally this can be done if:

- the deal was done in the last few days and
- the deal was not done over the phone, but was done with the lender or supplier directly, in person and
- you did not sign the agreement in the trader's business premises, including an exhibition stand

If the lender has not yet signed the agreement, you may be able to cancel the credit deal, even if the period allowed for cancellation has expired.

Although the goods may have arrived, you can still cancel if you are within the time limit set. You should get any deposit back.

## Early settlement

If you decide, partway through a loan, that you are able to pay it off early, you could get an early settlement rebate, which is a proportion of the charges outstanding.

If you want to pull out of a hire purchase agreement after the end of the cancellation period, you can only do so if you are up-to-date with your payments and have paid at least half the total amount owed. You must return the goods, and if they are damaged or in bad condition you may have to pay for repairs. You cannot sell goods bought on HP until the agreement has been paid off.

## Repossession of goods

Creditors can only repossess goods if they have been bought under a hire purchase or Conditional Sale agreement, in which case the finance company legally owns the goods until the final payment has been made. With nearly all other credit agreements you own the goods, and all that creditors can do is to start court action to recover their money.

In the case of hire purchase, if the company wants to stop the loan early because you have broken the agreement in some way (usually through falling behind with repayments), they have to give you seven days' advance warning with the chance to put things right. You can ask for more time through a court order if you wish.

If you have paid more than one-third of the total cost, the company will need a court order to recover the goods. If you have paid less than one-third, it does not need a court order; it cannot enter your home to recover the goods without your permission, or without a court order.

## Credit reference agencies

Credit reference agencies collect financial information about people and

### Guarantors

Sometimes, a lender may ask for there to be a guarantor in connection with a loan. This means that, if the borrower stops paying the loan, then the guarantor has to pay the amount outstanding. So, if you agree to act as a guarantor for someone else's loan, ensure that you see all the paperwork, to know what your liability might be, and only do so if you can afford to take the risk.

businesses. Their records will show credit companies if you are behind with existing payments, in arrears or have a county court judgement against you. They will show also when you have paid off any debt.

Credit companies and lenders, and also organisations like stockbrokers, will usually consult a credit reference agency over an application for credit. The check could result in a refusal to grant the credit. If you are denied credit, ask them (within 28 days) whether they used a credit reference agency, and which one. They are obliged to give you this information.

It is always a good idea to check with the credit reference agency in these circumstances, to see if there is a relevant entry about you on their files. To check their file on you, write to the credit reference agency involved with a cheque or postal order for £1. You will not get this money back. Give your full name, current address and any other address where you have lived in the previous six years.

When you have received your file, if you think there is an incorrect entry, write to the agency asking it to amend or remove the entry. You should use up to 200 words, preferably fewer, explaining the circumstances and the reason for correction. If the agency agrees to change your entry or add your notice of correction, it will send the details to everyone who has asked to see your file in the last six months. Write to the Director General of Fair Trading if the agency refuses to accept your notice of correction. Alternatively, you could contact the 'subscriber' (the organisation that submitted the entry) and ask them to put it right. If they refuse to do so, or are unhelpful, then contact the credit reference agency.

## DEBT PROBLEMS

If you find yourself getting into debt it is important to confront the problem and work out how to sort it out. The longer you leave it, the worse your difficulties will become, and you could find yourself losing some of your possessions, perhaps even losing your home.

- Work out what you need for normal living expenses, and what your income is, so that you know how much you can afford to put towards repaying your debts. Try to exclude 'luxuries' like cigarettes or drink, but don't be too mean about food and heating, especially where children are involved, and keep a small amount for emergencies.

- Identify what your debts are, and prioritise them. Mortgage and rent are important to sort out, or you could end up homeless. Also, utilities bills like gas, electricity or water need to be sorted out or these services could be cut off. Hire purchase goods can be repossessed without a court order if you have paid less than one-third of the cost.

- Tell your creditors that you are having problems with arrears, and explain how much you think you can repay them, and by when. Put your case in writing, giving the number of your credit agreement or bank account. Be honest about your circumstances, but never offer to pay more than you can manage. Ask the lender to consider freezing the interest payment, and seek their advice about the best way to pay.

- If you find a creditor is difficult, or refuses to accept your proposed payment plan, ask to speak to someone higher in the company. If you can demonstrate that you are genuinely trying to sort out your problems, most creditors will be helpful.

- It is always a good idea to start paying the amount you have offered as soon as possible, even if the creditor has not yet accepted your offer.

**Going to court**

If you cannot resolve your debt problem with a creditor, he or she may take you to court – which may not be as bad as it sounds. The county court will arbitrate between you and your creditor to decide what money is owed and how it should be repaid. It is not a criminal court.

The court will decide what will be fair for you to repay, and will stop any further interest being charged to your debt. If you do not agree with the court decision, you can ask for a hearing before the district judge, at which you can put your case in person, provided you apply within 14 days of the Court Order. A personal court appearance will not result in a report in your local paper.

The costs of a court case are added on to your debt. You must pay the monthly amount ordered or further action can be taken against you. If your circumstances change you can apply to the court for a reduction.

A county court judgement could well affect your credit rating, and you might find it hard to get credit until your debt has been repaid.

## Repossession and eviction

If you are taken to court as a result of mortgage arrears and the court does not accept your proposals for repaying the arrears, you can ask for an adjournment to give you time to sell the property rather than be evicted. If the court does not agree, you will normally have 28 days before the lender can take action about evicting you. If you need more time, or wish to make a new repayment offer, you can apply for a new court hearing.

The position is similar regarding rented accommodation. You can apply to the court to stop an eviction order if you need more time to be rehoused, or if you wish to make a new offer of repayment. Additionally, you can claim money from your landlord for repairs that they should have carried out and did not, for example, or if you have been made ill or your belongings damaged as a result of your landlord's negligence.

If you have an assured shorthold tenancy and it has come to an end, you cannot stay in your home. Otherwise, you cannot be evicted from a property without a court order. If the lender or your landlord starts threatening you or tries to evict you, seek professional help.

## Magistrates' court fines

A magistrates' court fine for, say, a parking offence, or not paying a television licence, can lead to mandatory deductions from your wages or income support, or even imprisonment if it is not paid, and so should be treated seriously. The amount of the fine is normally based on your income. If you have not made arrangements to pay the fine, the court may try to use bailiffs to seize your goods and sell them.

It is essential to attend all the court hearings required, to keep paying what you can afford, and to contact the court if you cannot pay. In exceptional circumstances the court can order that your fine be written off.

---

### Bullying or harassment

Don't let creditors persuade you to pay more than you can afford – this will reduce what you can pay your other creditors – or to bully or harass. This is illegal, and if it happens to you complain to your local Trading Standards Department, Consumer Protection Department, Citizens' Advice Bureau, or Money Advice Centre.

---

## Council Tax

If you fall into arrears with your Council Tax payments, try to come to an arrangement with your Council for an alternative payment scheme. If you cannot come to an arrangement, the Council will apply to the magistrates' court for a Liability Order. This allows the Council to take measures against you such as taking the arrears directly from your pay, or arranging for bailiffs to go to your home to take possessions to sell to pay the arrears. They can also secure the debt on your home, where it is more than £1,000, which could mean you lose your home eventually.

If you feel your Council Tax banding is incorrect, a Valuation Tribunal will consider your case. You should in the first place contact the Listing Officer for your area at the local office of the Valuation Office Agency, not your Council. (The address is on your Council Tax bill, or in the phone book under Valuation Office). The grounds for appeal are:

- where there has been a decrease in your home's value
- where you stop or start using part of your home to carry out a business, or the balance between business and domestic use changes
- where, following either of the above, the Listing Officer has altered a list without a proposal being made by a taxpayer

If you appeal to the Listing Officer but he does not agree with it, or if you cannot agree on an alternative or if no decision has been made at the end of six months, the Listing Officer must refer your proposal to a Valuation Tribunal. Valuation Tribunals are independent tribunals which are normally free, unless you choose to employ a solicitor. Hearings should last only a day, and the Tribunal's decision is final, though appeals on points of law can be made to the High Court.

## Bankruptcy

Bankruptcy can sometimes be unavoidable. People can declare themselves bankrupt voluntarily by contacting their local court, or a bankruptcy petition can be initiated by a creditor who is owed at least £750.

When a bankruptcy petition is made against you must:

- Give the official receiver full details of what you owe and what you own, including all your financial records. These are normally destroyed after they have been examined.
- Stop using your bank or building society accounts immediately. You may be allowed a new account so long as you tell the bank or building society that you are a bankrupt.
- You must not obtain credit.
- With a few exceptions, you must not make any repayments to your creditors directly.
- You must co-operate with anything the court asks you to do, or you could be arrested.

If you own your home, it will probably have to be sold. If you have a partner with interests in the home, they should take legal advice. A legal disposal of your interest may be arranged to give them rights to the house and prevent a forced sale at some future date.

You can keep equipment and sometimes vehicles needed to carry on your business, and also basic household items such as clothes, bedding and furniture. Everything else is controlled by the Trustee, who will sell the possessions to pay his fees and your creditors.

### About bailiffs

If you have a mortgage and know you are going to be evicted, you should try to move out before the day of repossession or the bailiffs can enter by force and without your permission. In rented accommodation, some landlords can arrange for a private bailiff to go into your home and take your possessions to sell to pay rent that may be owing. Bailiffs cannot enter your home by force unless you have let them in before. If bailiffs try to get in, contact a debt counselling service for advice immediately.

**After bankruptcy**

Discharge from bankruptcy is normally two but may be three years after the Bankruptcy Order, or when your debts have been paid in full. It does not necessarily mean that you are released from all your debts. Certain debts arising from crime, fraud or fines may be released only when the court sees fit. After bankruptcy you can borrow money, or carry on a business or be a Company Director.

For information and advice consult the Citizens' Advice Bureau, or write to the Law Society, or the DTI's Insolvency Service, which produces a useful *Guide to Bankruptcy*.

## GENERAL SOURCES OF HELP

The external bodies identified in this chapter as being appropriate to approach with a problem are not the only sources of assistance. Other people who may be able to help are:

- **Your local MP**, if the problem is in their constituency, or they can refer the matter to one of their colleagues in the government for them to look into the dispute. You should be able to get their contact address or phone number from the phone book, or from the local paper, or by ringing the House of Commons (0171 219 3000)
- **Your local MEP**, if your problem has a European connection – if you are having problems transferring money to a bank in the European Union for example. You can contact them through the local constituency party or by writing to them at the European Parliament, rue Belliard 97-113, 1040 Brussels, Belgium.
- **The Consumers' Association** Their *Which? Personal Service* provides legal advice and help to subscribers. The costs of joining the service are small, and their results can be impressive.
- **Consumer action groups** where there is a common injustice, such as misappropriation of pension funds.

# USEFUL ADDRESSES

The Association of British
Insurers
51 Gresham Street
London EC2V 7HQ
Telephone: 0171 600 3333

The Association of
Investment Trust Companies
Park House, 6th Floor
16 Finsbury Circus
London EC2M 7JJ
Telephone: 0171 588 5347

The Association of Unit Trust
and Investment Funds
65 Kingsway
London WC2B 6TD
Telephone: 0171 831 0898

Banking Ombudsman
70 Gray's Inn Road
London WC1X 8NB
Telephone: 0171 404 9944

The Birmingham Settlement
Telephone: 0121 359 8501

The British Bankers'
Association
10 Lombard Street
London EC3V 9EL
Telephone: 0171 623 4001

The Building Societies'
Association
3 Savile Row
London W1X 1AF
Telephone: 0171 437 0655

Building Societies'
Ombudsman
35-37 Grosvenor Gardens
London SW1X 7AW
Telephone: 0171 931 0044

The Chartered Institute of
Arbitrators (Personal
Insurance Arbitration Service)
24 Angel Gate
City Road
London EC1V 2RS
Telephone: 0171 837 4483

The Consumers' Association
(*Which? Personal Service*)
2 Marylebone Road
London NW1 4DF
Telephone: 0171 486 5544

Consumer Credit Counselling
Service
Wade House
Merrion Centre
Leeds LS2 8NG
Telephone: 01532 342202

The Council of Mortgage
Lenders (*see* Building
Societies' Association)

CREDIT REFERENCE
AGENCIES
Equifax Europe (UK) Ltd
Consumer Affairs Department
Spectrum House
1A North Avenue
Clydebank
Glasgow G81 2DR

Infolink Ltd
CCA Department
38 Whitworth Street
Manchester
M60 1QH

CCN Credit Systems
Consumer Affairs Department
PO Box 40
Nottingham NG7 2SS

Credit Data and Marketing
Services
CCA Department
Dove Mill
Dean Church Lane
Bolton
Lancs BL3 4ET

Director General of Fair
Trading
Field House
Bream's Buildings
London EC4A 1PR
Telephone: 0171 242 2858

The Inland Revenue
Adjudicator
Haymarket House, 3rd Floor
28 Haymarket
London SW1Y 4SP
Telephone: 0171 930 2565

The Insolvency Service
PO Box 203
21 Bloomsbury Street
London WC1B 3QW
Telephone: 0171 291 6740

The Insurance Ombudsman
City-Gate 1
135 Park Street
London SE1 9EA
Telephone: 0171 928 7600

Investment Management
Regulatory Organisation
(IMRO)
Broadwalk House
5 Appold Street
London EC2A 2LL
Telephone: 0171 628 6022

**The Investment Ombudsman**
6 Frederick's Place
London EC2R 8BT
Telephone: 0171 796 3065

**The Investor's Compensation
Scheme**
(same as SIB)

**The London Stock Exchange**
London EC2N 1HP
Telephone: 0171 797 1000

**National Association of CABs
(NACAB)**
115-123 Pentonville Road
London N1 9LZ
Telephone: 0171 833 2181

**Occupational Advisory
Service (OPAS)**
(*see* Pensions Ombudsman)

**The Pensions' Ombudsman**
11 Belgrave Road
London SW1 1RB
Telephone: 0171 834 9144

**Personal Investment
Authority (PIA)**
3-4 Royal Exchange Buildings
London EC3V 3NL
Telephone: 0171 929 0072

**Securities and Investments
Board (SIB)**
Gavrelle House
2-14 Bunhill Row
London EC1Y 8RA
Telephone: 0171 638 1240

**Shelter**
88 Old Street
London EC1V 9HU
Telephone: 0171 253 0202

# INDEX